DOCTOR THOMAS MONRO
1759-1833

Physician, Patron a

Note for Librarians: A cataloguing record for this book is available from Library
and Archives Canada at www.collectionscanada.ca/amicus/index-e.html

Printed in Victoria, BC, Canada.

ISBN: 978-1-4120-9973-8 (sc)

*Our mission is to efficiently provide the world's finest, most comprehensive
book publishing service, enabling every author to experience success.
To find out how to publish your book, your way, and have it available
worldwide, visit us online at www.trafford.com*

Trafford rev. 8/26/2009

www.trafford.com

North America & international
toll-free: 1 888 232 4444 (USA & Canada)
phone: 250 383 6864 ♦ fax: 812 355 4082

Diary for Dr Thomas Monro

CONTENTS

Portrait of Dr Thomas Monro by Henry Monro

This book is dedicated to my aunt Elmire Wade
It was her lifetime project which she never had time to complete

DOCTOR THOMAS MONRO 1759-1833

Physician, Patron and Painter

INTRODUCTION

Thomas Monro, art collector and doctor to the insane, was a unique figure in London society of the eighteenth and early nineteenth centuries. In his professional capacity as head of Bethlem Hospital, or Bedlam, the Hospital for the Insane, he was summoned to treat George the third, during his bouts of madness. His private passion was painting in watercolour, and amongst the artists he befriended and encouraged were J.M.W. Turner and Thomas Girtin.

Monro appears to be the missing link in the change of style in watercolours that took place around the beginning of the nineteenth century. Many young men who became leading artists of their day were students at the informal meeting of artists held in his house on Adelphi Terrace, weekly on a Friday evening, from 1794. His house became a studio turning out endless sketches and coloured drawings by artists, known as "Monro School Copies". They copied from drawings by Monro, J.R.Cozens, William Alexander, Henry Edridge and Thomas Hearn: also Monro's neighbour John Henderson had a known contemporary collection of drawings, as had Monro himself, from which the students copied. In addition to Turner and Girtin, John Linnell, John Sell Cotman, Peter de Wint, William Henry Hunt, Joshua Cristall and John Varley, among others, found their way to Monro's evening gatherings. Monro and his friends taught them accuracy in drawing, accompanying them on outdoor sketching trips, teaching them to see from Nature, as well as giving them the enjoyment of the company of other young artists, with an opportunity to share ideas. The as yet, unacknowledged Monro, played a key role in the development of the styles of these artists. The rise and establishment of watercolour painting, with the standards and ideals which Monro insisted upon, had much to do with the unrivalled position which the English School in Water-Colours had attained by the time of his death, whilst John Ruskin went so far as to say that Thomas Monro was "Turner's true master".

Many papers are still held by family members, which is why so little correct information has appeared on Thomas Monro to date. With five children surviving him, much has been distributed to their descendants, so it is difficult to get a clear picture. Included in the story is a brief description of Bedlam, or the Bethlem Hospital. Monro never kept a diary, but his son Edward Thomas (Tom) did, and these diaries and those of his artistic son Henry, and Sally his daughter, have been made available to me. These form the basis for the book and are held by a member of the family. Letters and descriptions, many still in private hands, give furtherinsight

CHAPTER 1 – FORMATIVE YEARS

Descended from the Fyrish branch of the ancient Scottish family of Munro of Fowlis, Thomas Monro occupied a position in the history of British painting in watercolour which was unique. He happened to come on the scene at a very critical moment, having been born in 1759 - at a time when this branch of art was beginning to assert itself. He was by heredity and natural tendency romantic, enthusiastic and quite unconventional. He inherited from his father, Dr. John Monro, a good position as a Physician of Madness at Bethlem Hospital, and in his profession, occupied various official positions in the Royal College, and was one of the eminent physicians called in on the case of King George III. Yet all his life it seems to have been art and not science, which was at first a hobby and then became a passion, since he was an artist himself with a keen appreciation of beauty, and a great interest in depicting Nature. Unusual for his day, he seems not to have cared whether his friends and the students with whom he surrounded himself were well or humbly born, so long as they could show a love of beauty and pursue art with reverence and determination. He grew up in his father's house in Red Lyon Square, Holborn, which was filled with prints and drawings.

The Monro family were not people of Fashion, but representative of the growing class of intelligentsia, interested in education but still of the 'gentleman' class, living on the fringes of the artistic world. Theatre, Literature and Art were all a part of their world. At this time the English were beginning to look at nature through different eyes - the eyes of the poet and the artist, as the landscape watercolour grew out of the tradition of topography, or the landscape of the place, and artists became gradually caught up in the interest in light. For the most advanced and avant garde of their day the picturesque, showing terror-inspiring precipitous crags and awe-inspiring rural beauty, in many ways was exemplified by the work of Monro's two pupils, J.M.W. Turner and Thomas Girtin, who followed the lead of their contemporaries. Paul Sandby, one of the public spirited men who was behind the establishment of the Royal Academy, often called the father of English watercolour, perfected the more topographical aspect, as did Edward Dayes, the short term tutor to Girtin. Many writers tended to belittle the efforts of the art before Turner, as though it consisted entirely of pen and ink outline drawings, washed with monochrome and then gently coloured, but they forgot about John Robert Cozens, whose drawings were to inspire not only Thomas Monro, the patron, but also his young protégés.

Thomas Monro became a great lover of art, as well as a collector of drawings. He was the third generation of the Monro family to become known for the treatment of insanity, but in addition he became an amateur artist and collector, who encouraged young men who showed promise in the rising school of watercolour. He was an excellent draftsman, a pupil of John Laporte, and both men were keen followers of Gainsborough's style in landscapes and drawing. Monro loved to escape to sketch outdoors whenever he found time in his busy life. His patronage of young artists at the turn of the century, was that he brought them together at his house, not only to have access to his pictures and many portfolios of drawings, but also to encourage them by giving them access to the advice of his artistic friends, as well as his own opinions. This would have been of considerable importance to them at a time when there were few opportunities for young artists to study. Monro accompanied several of them into the countryside, encouraging them to sketch from Nature, showing them methods of capturing light and movement in watercolour. A few of the best watercolour painters benefited from their early practice at Dr. Monro's, the most distinguished being J.M.W. Turner and Thomas Girtin, who will ever be linked together as the real founders of the British school of watercolours.

Thomas Monro was the youngest son of a doctor in lunacy, and the family, though comfortably off, were not possessed of great wealth. It can, therefore, hardly be supposed that in those days his position would have been conducive to his moving, as he did, in the artistic and intellectual milieu of London, had it not been that he had an unusual personality, also gifts which charmed and at least interested his contemporaries to some degree. His father John was a great collector of prints and Thomas grew up with an appreciation and understanding of fine art, which accompanied his artistic personality. The family was traditionally associated with medicine, but Thomas, as the fourth son, never had any expectations initially, of entering the medical profession.

His great-grandfather Alexander, born in 1648, was originally one of the Munros from Fowlis. He became Professor of Divinity at St. Andrews in 1682, and then Principal of Edinburgh University. He was also Minister of the High Kirk of St. Giles and titular Bishop of Argyll. He had strong leanings towards the cause of James 11, and was deprived of his posts as he refused to sign the oath of allegiance when, with William of Orange, the Presbyterians came to power. He was deposed, and put in prison, when it was suggested that he had been plotting against the King. Alexander was eventually released, and went south to London. He lived in very humble circumstances, even being imprisoned in Newgate for five months. His estates in Scotland were eventually taken from him. He owned an estate known as Fyrish whilst his kinsman, Hector Munro, owned an estate alongside, Novar. Hector had no love for the Jacobite Alexander, and finally succeeded in depriving him of the lands, by waylaying the post and taking his letters. Under Scottish law at that time, an absentee landlord, abandoning his estates, could be obliged to forfeit his lands, and this seems to have been the case here. Alexander, in London, changed the spelling of his name to Monro, registering a new coat of arms in 1687. His wife not only wrote to his solicitor whilst he was in Scotland, but seems to have struggled to keep in touch with relatives, in order to keep the family going in London. Alexander managed a poor living, writing controversial books and pamphlets. He wrote at this time "my lodging so uncertain I cannot inform you how to direct a letter -", and his letter was sent from the White Bear at Billingsgate.[1] Alexander died in London in 1698.

The Bishop's son James, who was aged eleven in 1691 when the family came to London, was sent to Balliol College, Oxford, with family help, and became a Fellow of the Royal College of Physicians in 1722. He was appointed to the Royal Bethlem Hospital in 1728. Letters from James, addressed to Mr. John Mackenzie of Delvine, who seems to have acted in an advisory capacity, were rediscovered in a cupboard, a couple of hundred years after they were written, by a butler at the Mackenzie's old estate, then owned by the Muir family. The 'Delvin papers' indicate that James struggled to put his affairs in order. He wrote:

Oxford Sept. ye 17 1708

"My Mother some time ago informed that Fyres (by ye death of my Uncles and their children) now fell to me, and ye other day I had a letter from my Uncle Hugh to that effect... He tells me that a very little matter would soon clear ye Estate".... I have written to ye Laird of Fouls to befriend in anthing of this metter that may ly in his poure: and I have no reason to dout your Kindness, to Sir

Yr. most obliged and most humble Servant   Ja. Monro"[2]

Fyrish remained in the Monro family, coming through the direct line to Thomas Monro's older brother Capt. James Heics, the second son of Doctor John, and then to his son James.

John, born in November 1715, son of James and grandson to Alexander, went to St. John's College at Oxford, and on going down was appointed, like his father James, to "Bedlam", the Bethlem Hospital, initially as Medical Registrar, where his treatment of insanity gave him greater eminence than that of his father. John's contemporaries included the renowned pioneer psychiatrist, William Battie, M.D., F.R.C.S., who appears to have carried on continuous warfare against Dr. John Monro. Despite his established reputation as a doctor in lunacy, the treatment at Bethlem had limitations, imposed by the Governors, and Dr. John Monro appears to have made few alterations during his lifetime. The post of Chief Physician at Bethlem became practically hereditary, and was held in due course by five members of the Monro family in succession.

Charles Dickens describes the situation in 1750, when "Bethlem Hospital was a dry walk for loiterers and a show, where they were chained naked, in rows of cages that flanked a promenade and were jeered at through iron bars by London loungers and half a dozen gentlemen met together to found a new asylum for the insane." Dickens here is referring to St. Lukes, founded at this time, presided over by Dr. Battie. In 1758, when Dr. Battie's treatise on madness was published, Dr. John Monro, found it necessary to retaliate to this document. "I felt it was necessary to say something in my situation in answer to the undeserved censures which Dr. Battie has thrown on my predecessors, although my inclination would never have led me to appear in print." It is recorded that Monro's book perfectly affected its object, and covered Dr. Battie with what then seemed to be well-merited ridicule. There is perhaps a trace

5

of Highland realism in one of John Monro's objections to the policy pursued at St. Luke's. He could see no use in "enquiry into matters so far out of our reach as the *causes* of madness. Let us direct our knowledge to relieve them, leaving causes of this terrible calamity to such as can fancy there is any amusement in a disquisition of so unpleasant a nature." He also says that those who have been so happy as to recover from this state describe it no otherwise than a total suspension of every rational faculty.[3] He sounds a practical man. He also had a large private practice in lunacy, since he started a private lunatic asylum, Brook House, which was inherited by his son Thomas, then to Edward Thomas, and then to his son Henry. It was destroyed by bombs in 1940. There was also another private 'safe house' in Clerkenwell. He was one of the officials attending Bridewell prison.

There is a reference to one of the Monros in the Dunciad, of which Alexander Pope published a definitive version in 1743. Although attributed to Dr. John Monro, it would by date, have originally been meant for his father, Doctor James, the first of the family to become a physician at Bethlem Hospital, (1680-1752). His policy of not admitting students or physicians to the practice of his hospital was subject to hostile criticism by his contemporary Dr. Battie. John was also referred to as 'a skilful and honourable physician.', but was still at Oxford in 1742, where he took his degree in 1747, and his FRCP in 1753. These four lines of Pope's ran:-

> "Close to those walls, where folly holds her throne
> And laughs to think Monro would take her down
> Where o'er the gates, by his famed father's hand
> Great Cibber's brazen,brainless brothers stand."

'Folly holding her throne' was referring to the Rag Fair, which was held weekly against the walls of Bethlem hospital. 'Cibber' refers to the two statues either side of the front gate, by Caius Cibber (1630-1700), depicting *Melancholy* and *Raving Madness.* These can be clearly seen in an oval picture in the old Board Room of the Coram Foundation, where a series of pictures illustrate the London Hospitals of the early 1700's. At this time there was also a well known actor and dramatist, Colley Cibber (1671-1757) who became known for his role in *Melancholy and Raving Madness,* a popular play by mid-century, which could also prove an appropriate reference in this instance.

From his sale catalogue, we know that John Monro had a considerable collection of engravings and prints, and was also a friend of Hogarth, who gave him several engravings and two of his pictures. John Monro had allowed Hogarth to be shown around Bethlem Hospital, where he made many sketches, to be used by him for his series *The Rake's Progress.* Whilst at Oxford John had received the Radcliffe travelling fellowship, an appointment tenable for ten years, which involved his travelling through France, Germany, Italy and Holland, where he studied medicine at Leyden. All this travelling must have given him ample opportunity for learning and observing, and was no doubt the primary inspiration for his becoming a collector of engravings and works of art. To this day his descendants own several oil paintings he acquired when travelling through Europe, one or two reputed to be from the collection of Charles 1.[7] A sale of his collection of engravings, sketches and drawings was advertised to take place on April 30, 1792, to last for two days, which in fact lasted for five. It was listed as containing: 'A great number of the most ancient Engravings from the earliest period of the Art to the present time - to include sketches and drawings.' The sale realised a total amount of £896.6s. a goodly sum in those days. The catalogue was of immense length, including many famous names, with portfolios of drawings by Teniers, Ovid's Metamorphoses and many other books of prints. The

7

drawings presented to Monro by Hogarth were sold, and prints presented to him by this artist included *The Lake of Albano* by Claude, engraved by LaPorte, and a portrait of Erasmus by Holbein.[8] This perhaps indicates where the interests of Dr. John lay, and how his taste may have influenced his son Thomas Monro. In 1803 Thomas Monro told Joseph Farington that he had inherited from his father an inclination for drawings, but it is evident he had his own tastes and set out to eventually build his own collection of drawings, which included many sketches and drawings by his pupils. His father's collection probably lacked the emotional appeal that was, in due course, to stir the heart of Thomas, especially when he came across some of the young talented painters in watercolour. The formidable list of important artistic personalities covering 250 years, ends with eighty one Guerchinos by Bartolozzi, so we know they must have been prints, described as "the finest impressions and in the best condition". Twenty-two ancient frontispieces confirm the suggestion that a number of these prints must have come out of books. The fourth day of the sale ended with twelve lots of Hogarth's works, whilst "pictures and drawings framed and glazed" sold on the fifth day, must have formed the cream of the collection.[9]

There are several letters in existence showing that John Monro must have been a generous man, as seen in a letter from Hugh Munro of Dalmore who wrote to his kinsman in the South, in May, 1772, asking for his help with his fifteen year old son, and various other members of the family. The letter seems to have brought help, since in 1773, he thanks him for the five guineas sent. Another letter in 1775, comes from Sir Harry Munro writing:

Fowlis Castle

"In the situation I am in as head of our Clan, it is my duty and inclination to do all I can for the welfare of my kinsfolk and to rejoice when I hear they are sober and diligent. I have particular concern in the young man I mention (Hugh Munro's son) and do return you my best thanks for the notice you have taken of him and intreat the continuance of your good offices. Lady Munro regrets much she was not so lucky as to have had an acquaintance in your family when she was in town winter '73 but hopes for that pleasure next time we come to London. Accept of her compls. toe Mrs. Monro and yourself..........." He ends the letter:

Dear Sir, Yours most, obedt. sevt. & cousin Harry Munro.

Hugh Munro writes again to Dr. John Monro, on 17th January, 1776, thanking him for his kindness to his son John:

"The continuance of yur salutary advice and good offices to my son while in London is a means of rendering me unspeakably indebted and uncommonly obliged to yur favors and goodness." These letters indicate that Doctor John, the father of Thomas Monro, was on good terms with the other side of his family, the Munros, and was also of a kindly character.[10] He died in 1791, at the age of seventy six, being 'endowed with an elegant taste, and his collections of books and of prints was very considerable. Deeply versed in the early history of engraving, he gave great help to Strutt in his work on that subject,'" we are told by Roget. He was installed as Candidate of the College of Physicians on 25th June, 1752, and was a Fellow by 25th June, 1753 He is said to have attained greater success on the treatment of insanity than any of his contemporaries. Although he was attacked by paralysis in 1783, and his strength began to decline, he kept on with his profession. It was John Monro who stopped the practise of indiscriminate visiting of wards at Bedlam by the general public, and with John Winder, the Apothecary, they insisted on improvements in the wards which made for greater privacy and comfort for the patients. As a doctor this reflects his humane interests, but medically he seems not to have advanced the actual treatment of the insane.

Thomas Monro was born on June 29th, 1759. From the little reliable existing information and from what is known of the Monro family at a later time, it is possible to conjecture that much care and time was spent on the training of the eldest son John, whose destiny it was thought would be to succeed his father at Bedlam, and that young Thomas may well have developed a feeling of inferiority. He had an older brother James, Captain and later owner of the merchant ship *Houghton,* trading with China. His second brother, the third son, was Charles, who became a solicitor. Another son Culling died in infancy, whilst a sister Charlotte, who was the youngest, reputed to have been a beautiful girl, died at the age of twenty one, unmarried.. Thomas was sent to Harrow at a tender age, since the custom of sending boys to public schools very young went on until well after the middle of the nineteenth century. Harrow, granted a charter by Queen Elizabeth in 1571, was originally intended as a free grammar school for local boys, but was soon allowed to take boarders. During the nineteenth century, with the broadening of the curriculum beyond Latin and Greek, it developed into one of the great public schools, beginning to be patronised by the aristocracy late in the eighteenth century, and during the Victorian period became a school patronised by the middle class intelligentsia.   As a very young and sensitive boy, Thomas was taught by Dr. Samuel Parr, (1747-1825) who had himself been at Harrow, and had a reputation for a fiery temper. Parr was ambitious, and having left school in 1761 at the age of fourteen, seems to have offered himself for the post of Headmaster at an early age, favouring education rather than medicine as a career, but was turned down owing to his youth. However, in 1766, Robert Sumner who had succeeded Thackeray to the post, offered Parr the place of first assistant at £50. per annum, which he accepted. Parr was also ordained deacon by the Bishop of London at this time. Having studied under the literary background of Thackeray, Parr in turn became responsible for teaching Richard Brinsley Sheridan, which may have been a contributory reason for Thomas Monro and his family having been keenly interested in the stage. Parr was not reputed to have much in the way of gracious manners or kindness according to Samuel Rogers, but in fact was well known for his temper, and managed to offend the Governors by opposing their claim to order holidays at discretion. Parr's own account is that he voted for Wilkes in the Middlesex election and was asked to leave. As a result Parr started a rival school at Stanmore, in October 1771, and took forty of his former scholars with him, including Thomas Monro. It is of special interest that he should have written a most kind letter to his ex-pupil from Norwich, where he later taught at the Grammar School there

Norwich   Jan. 22nd — no year —

To Mr. Thomas Monro, at Dr. Monro's, Red Lion Square
"Thank you much for your very sensible and proper letter, - it is always agreeable to me to hear from such of my scholars as have distinguished themselves by their regularity, their diligence, & their liberal sentiments. I was t'other day favoured with a very judicious letter from your cousin's mother . . . .

11

Depend on my faithful and most tender affection to your cousin to whom I shall hold up your example with pleasure & I hope with effect.

I beg my best compliments to your family and as your relatives live in this part of the world, I shall hope to welcome you under my roof at Norwich and believe me with every sincere regard, dear Sir,

Yours,   S. Parr[12]

This letter may be very revealing as to the manners of Dr. Parr at his best, and of the qualities of Thomas Monro seen through the eyes of his schoolmaster and described by his pen. The relative, who was at the Norwich Grammar School, also called Thomas Monro (1764-1815), was eventually ordained and known to have been joint author of a series of diverting essays entitled *Olla Poedrida*. He writes in the style of Dr. Johnson's *Idler* (1787), popular at that time, perhaps more in youthful jest than in earnest:

"In my attempts to collect materials I shall hope to succeed notwithstanding Oxford (according to the opinion of many) is such a dull, insipid, out of the way place, that if it were not for the stage coaches, it would be difficult for a body to pick up news enough in the week to furnish a petit-maitre's pocket book." Dr. Johnson himself, in the *Idler* speaks of the 'genius of the place', but changes his view in August 1775, when Oxford is described as "the place is now a sullen solitude." Many years later, on an evening in December, 1795, Monro recalled Parr, and the reason why he left Harrow. Joseph Farington, at that time secretary to the Royal Academy members and keeper of a detailed diary, was dining with the Monros. It was a large party including Mrs. Monro's sister, a Mrs. Hardy, married to Captain Hardy, and three friends. Farington recalled Monro describing the 'singularities of Parr. "Sometimes for a fortnight together He would lay late in bed and pay little regard to the School which of course became relaxed in discipline. He would then suddenly change his habit, rise at 6 in the morning, and with great severity force on his instruction." These irregularities caused the school to decline. From thence he went to Colchester: and from thence to Norwich. Lord Dartmouth gave him a living in Warwickshire, where being settled He took in a number of boys at £100 a year each. This plan he continues. Dr. Monro says that in his conversation he is sententious, like Johnson: and expresses himself in a very powerful manner on all subjects that he speaks upon. He is a man of uncouth appearance: and is remarkable for looking much older than He is in reality. He cannot now be more than 46 years old, yet appears at least 60". [13] By 1802 Sir Francis Burdett, friend to Sheridan, had offered Parr a rectory in Huntingdonshire which was in his gift, with the motive behind this gift "that I cannot do anything more pleasing to —Mr. Fox, Mr Sheridan and Mr. Knight." Parr obviously had friends or ex-pupils in many high places."[14]

Thomas Monro then went to Oriel College, Oxford, for a period of ten years, acquiring his DM. on 24th May, 1787. There are few letters or details giving any information of his life here, so it is not known what his initial studies were, although there is evidence that he came under the tuition of Dr. Lightfoot of Merton (of which college Thomas's son Henry did a sketch, now in the Ashmolean Museum, Oxford.) The sudden death of John, the eldest brother, was to change any ideas Thomas may have held towards devoting his life to art. He stayed on at Oxford to qualify in medicine. John seems to have died very suddenly, early in 1779. Thomas took positive action by writing to his father offering to take up medicine in place of his deceased brother. There may have been two motives behind this, the first a sense of duty to do all that he could, the second a wish to prove to his father that he could be as valuable and effective as his elder brothers were.

There appears little doubt that a special relationship existed between Dr. John Monro and his eldest son John, since they shared an interest in medicine, and there is no doubt that Thomas was aware of this. There was a letter written in 1776, including a sketch, in which the father hopes his son's coming to London will not be deferred "and to incite to it if tardy I have enclosed you a rude sketch of a female infant, which I this day saw born with two complete heads. You may see the original of it and the dissection of it on Tuesday if in town. This obviously implies, not only that Jack, as he was called, was intended to follow as a physician in his father's footsteps, but that his father is fully aware of Jack's natural inclination towards medicine, and discussed interesting cases with him. A note which John sent to Thomas, was the last note that he ever wrote, and was obviously carried about in Thomas' pocket until it became dog-eared and grimy, with much sorrow and affection, which is witnessed by its very triviality, but it was obviously of great value to the recipient. It ran:

Dear Tom:

I shall be obliged to you if you will walk to St. John's some day this week and desire Bet Wilson my bed-maker to get my Bed ready against Friday seven-nights as I intend being in Oxford that evening.

I am, Yrs. sincerely,

John Monro

Another letter, dated July 7th, 1779, written in the neat hand of Charles Monro to his brother Thomas, states that he is writing rather than personally informing" his brother

"when we lost our poor brother Jack you with great kindness immediately offered yourself to take up that study which, had he been permitted to continue among us, he was pursuing. I feel the kindness of the offer but must own I was sorry you had made it as it was what I had intended to have done myself as soon as I thought my father sufficiently recovered from the Grief occasioned by the loss of poor Jack." (illus.) He goes on that he has now written to his father and that "the reasons which induce me to make an application now are many. In the first place from being much older than you, I think I shall be much sooner able to assist my father than yourself. I don't mean to insinuate that I have any chance of making a quicker progress in the knowledge of the art than you do, but the world seems to think age an indispensable qualification in a Physician. Add to this the thorough and unconquerable dislike I have to the practise of the law, a dislike which, however, I have hitherto kept to myself. At the same time the idea of practising Physic having necessarily been a very short time entertained by you make me hope that you will not look upon it as a disappointment should my father be inclined to agree to my wishes."

Charles' disapproval of his younger brother's offer was backed up, though in a gentler way, by their sister Charlotte, who considered Thomas to be too sensitive and vulnerable for the profession of medicine. Dr. John Monro accepted his son Thomas's offer despite these contrary views of his brother and sister, but family closeness was not ultimately harmed. Whatever resentment one brother might feel against the other did not last, and at the time of Charles' own illness and death in the early 1820's daily bulletins reached Dr. Thomas from various members of Charles' family, recording his state of health almost from hour to hour.

Thomas's older brother James, who served with the East India Company seems in his later years to have frequently visited at Thomas's country house Bushey, with his second wife Jane, and various children. He came to live at Hadley, a house that remained in the Monro family for 150 years. However at the time of John or Jack's death, James was away in the Far East. There are many references in the diary of Thomas Monro's eldest son, Edward Thomas, listing visits from Uncle Charles, and the younger cousins seem to have been close. His brother James's children also came to visit at Bushey after 1809. Meanwhile Thomas inherited the role of Mental Physician, which by his own ability he enhanced to no small degree, becoming principal physician at Bethlem Hospital by 1792. Although he became a leader in his profession, and occupied various official positions in the Royal College, where his portrait by his second son Henry now hangs, and was one of the physicians called in to treat King George III, 'yet all the time there is no doubt that it was art and not science that was the true mistress of his life.[16] 'He was an artist through and through, with a keen appreciation of beauty.' His great grandson continues the description:

> 'As an illustration of the Doctor's enthusiasm for Art one can hardly refrain from mentioning the story that has been so often told, how in his later days he had a net fixed in the roof of his brougham so that he could always have a drawing or a print at hand to look at as he drove from Bushey to London or the other way. This was very characteristic. He loved to surround himself with beautiful drawings. My mother, who was his granddaughter, has often described to me the manner in which he would cover the walls of his room at Bushey (his country house) with sketches by Gainsborough, Turner, Girtin and others. These sketches he pasted on to the wall side by side, neither mounted nor framed, and he would nail up strips of gilt beading to divide the one from the other and give the appearance of frames.'

The account of the Sale that took place at his death, shows that he had what was then a very remarkable collection both of drawings, prints and engravings by recognized masters. The fact that this collection was in his possession had a great deal to do with the help he was able to give to young artists. It included a very considerable number of landscape sketches by Gainsborough, as well as that artist's camera obscura "with ten subjects of landscapes, seapieces and moonlight." There were also several of Gainsborough's sketch books. Then there were large numbers of drawings by Cozens and T. Hearne and Dayes, and by Wilson and Paul Sandby. Canaletto, Rembrandt, Ostade, Paul Potter, Vandervelde, Mompert and Boucher were represented. There were sketches of Italian buildings by Claude, and a landscape in pen and ink by Titian. In addition to these there were many drawings and paintings by lesser men as well as very large numbers of prints of various kinds. All this wealth of material was placed at the disposal of the artists who were fortunate enough to study under his roof'[17]

It seems necessary to mention these facts at the beginning of a description of Monro's career since it points out several facts from his early life, indicating that he inherited many interests from his father, being at the same time enthusiastic and enthralled by the science of painting in watercolour, which was undergoing a rapid rise in interest and popularity during his early years. The Age of Enlightenment, bringing a renewed interest in nature, not to mention an interest in poetry and literature and the poets description of the English countryside, combined with the new vogue for the Picturesque and the Sublime, would all have been of fascination to a man we know to have been clever, a good student and involved with the literary world. Apart from an early interest in the theatre, Monro would have been very aware of leading writers and playwrights, moving as he did within the artistic circle in London. He himself had a wonderful gift of loyal friendship and

17

affectionate sympathy as will be seen, so that he appears as a quite unconventional man, with gifts peculiarly fitted for the part he was destined to play. As an amateur and besides a busy doctor there was no need for him to devote himself to young students, which he seems to have done against the wishes of his wife. He did so because he was fascinated in their work and interested in the drawing, and in watercolours. Today, it would seem a great waste that so many of his drawings, and those of his friends and students, were pasted on the wall and not treated with greater respect.

"Exactly how Monro chose his students is not clear, but he proved again and again, in his choice, that he had a sharp eye for talent, and having singled out his protégés, gave them generous encouragement".[18] He certainly became known, by the turn of the century, as a most serious patron of artists painting in watercolour. Roget's description tells us that "he himself was an able amateur draftsman, a pupil of Laporte's and an ardent sketcher, as well as worshipper of art." He continues the description: "There chanced to be an amateur whose fine and cultivated taste and practical knowledge, combined with a warm-hearted spirit of benevolence, and an earnest desire to foster a rising school of which he discerned the promise of excellence, enabled him about this time to do a most essential service to some young aspirants in this branch of art. This was Dr. Thomas Monro, already mentioned as the kind friend in need to John Cozens during the affliction under which that artist ended his days. As a leader of connoisseurship, he was looked upon in his day much in the same light as Sir George Beaumont and Mr. Payne Knight —none seem to have taken more effectual means to promote the education of young artists than Dr. Thomas Monro."[19]

Monro himself as a draughtsman rarely strayed outside monochrome, and the few coloured drawings attributable to him reveal black chalk as the basis for a very muted and mellow watercolour wash. In his style of sketching he was strongly influenced by Gainsborough, who was said to have been a personal friend, although Monro must have been very young if this was the case. Gainsborough died in 1788, a year after Thomas left Oxford and had begun to practise medicine. Certainly Monro held Gainsborough in great esteem, and it is not easy, even for an expert, to say for certain which are his drawings and which are the great artist's work. Perhaps the influence came partly from his teacher, John Laporte (1761-1839) described as an' English landscape painter, chiefly in water-colour,' by Redgrave,' who had a considerable practice as a drawing master'. Laporte was a frequent visitor to Adelphi Terrace, after the family moved there. He made soft ground etchings of Gainsborough's drawings, of which Monro had a large number. Monro during his lifetime meanwhile, witnessed an enormous change in style, with a new appreciation for landscape paintings in watercolour. There is no doubt he helped to foster this change, since so many of the contemporary artists were at one time students of his, at his Friday evening meetings. The change from topography in watercolour to pure landscapes, and the fascination with light, can be traced within the space of Dr. Monro's life from such painters as Thomas and Paul Sandby, also Francis Towne, who had much of the topographer about their work, through to Thomas Hearne, a good friend of Monro's, who helped with the young students of an evening. The diverse early talents of such as Turner and Girtin, closely following the influence of J.R. Cozens through Monro, also the crippled William Henry Hunt, apprenticed to John Varley, all worked with Monro, who recognised their talents. It would seem that although little is known of the formative years of the doctor, that his education shaped the man and his interest in the art and literature of his period, whilst many of his chosen students went on to become leading professional artists.

1. From a *Family History* written by G.K. Monro, for private circulation
2. Taken from copies of letters in G.K. Monro's *History*
3. *The History of Bedlam* The enquiry into the state of lunatics of the period
4. *The Works of Alexander Pope* Wordsworth Editions Ltd. Ware. Herts. 1995 Ed. p 142
5. *Bethlem Hospital, 1746* Painting by Edward Haytley - Collec. Of Coram Foundation
6. For catalogue contents see Monro file at the British Museum-Dept. of Prints c.167
7. A Cavalier of 1638, (Monro family) in the Dutch manner, painter unknown
8. Jefferiss, F.G. *Biography of Dr. Thomas Monro* typed & bound by V&A National Art Library. Appendix 1 - see also 1976 Exhibition Cat. For Monro Exh. at the V&A
9. Monro Catalogue - sale contents
10. Extracts from letters quoted are taken from a private collection. These were in the possession of Mrs. Dorothy Curtis Hayward. Further documents belonged to Mrs. Athelstan Coode, mother of Dorothy C-H. Coode papers
11. given to British Museum. Letters and a picture belonging to late W. Foxley Norris, Dean of York, grea grandson, are in the Gallery of Fine Arts, Cambridge, Mass. USA
12. Roget *History of the Old Water-Colour Society* Vol. 1 p77
13. Private letters in the collection of the Curti-Hayward family
14. Joseph Farington Diary - edited by Kenneth Garlic, 1978 p420
15. O'Toole, Fintan, *A Traitors' Kiss* Granta Books 1998 p408
16. Authors' collection
17. Foxley Norris, D.D., Article written for an exhibition of Bushey Artists
18. Ibid, see also article by the Old Water Colour Society Club, published 1924 Files now in British Museum (press mark ccl67.b.26.27)
19. Wilton, Andrew *British Watercolours 1750-1850* p30
20. Roget, *History of the Old Water Colour SocietyVol.l* pp77-79

CHAPTER 2 – MONRO AS PATRON

Thomas Monro, inspired initially by his family background, not only took an interest in collecting engravings, drawings and other works of art, but acquired the reputation as an artist by producing mainly grey washed or tinted drawings. Little is known about the doctor and the key role he played as a change of taste came about at the beginning of the nineteenth century, because so many papers and letters concerning him remain in various family hands. He had developed a cultivated taste, and a good artistic knowledge, which combined with a warm-hearted spirit of benevolence, led him to foster a rising school of young watercolour painters. Monro did not keep a diary until old age, and when he began his journal he wrote that he regretted not having kept one, so although the diary of his son Edward Thomas is helpful, it does not begin in any detail until 1806. It therefore must remain a mystery as to how he chose to patronise some of the young men who attended his evening seminars, although the stories of his initial friendship with J.M.W. Turner and Thomas Girtin have been recorded in various other journals, which leads to an understanding as to how they were chosen to assist the Doctor.

The most important years of the Monro Academy begin in 1794, when John Robert Cozens was assigned to Monro's care by Sir George Beaumont. At this time Cozens was in a complete state of 'nervous' collapse', or presumably on the verge of a nervous breakdown, having always been of a gentle personality. He was already known for his sensitive landscapes in watercolour, with some of his skills inherited from his father Alexander, and others acquired from travel in the Alps and Italy, in the company of William Beckford. Many of his surviving drawings were done in black chalk, with highlights in white, on prepared blue grey paper, and sometimes given a wash in pale green or yellow, but importantly taken directly from nature. In the last two years before his collapse he painted a series of English scenes in a soft misty light, with a large expanse of sky. Seeing his work, Monro seems to have been set alight with excitement, and determined to reproduce his work if he could. In a world where he knew Beaumont and shared several mutual friends, including Joseph Farington, Secretary to the Royal Academy, and Thomas Hearne, already an engraver and artist of note, as well as a loyal friend to Monro, he may have sought their advice. One of the sources of information is John Lewis Roget, in his History of the Old Water-Colour Society, who refers to Monro as patron of water-colour artists.

John Robert Cozens started on his career from observing the work of his father Alexander, art master at Eton College, and one of the pioneers of design in landscape drawing. His son revealed to many for the first time the mystical beauty of light and shade, revealing the forms and colours of the landscape. He was in Rome in 1776, and as early as 1778 he was not well. He resided in Rome with a Signor Martinelli, a Roman of good family but in reduced circumstances. Thomas Jones, who was there at the time refers to him as "little Cozens, the landscape painter". He was not strong enough to walk about much but rode about "on a jackass", and was sometime accompanied by Jones on a pony, which suggests that he was not well enough to undertake painting expeditions on foot. However he returned to England in April of the following year, taking with him his sketches. These persuaded the wealthy William Beckford to take him with him to Europe, and he is said to have made ninety two sketches for him, before falling ill and being left in Naples. Travelling with Beckford and his retinue of servants, with tutor and music master as well, was possibly exhausting, with Beckford himself very exacting in the manner of rich men, perhaps leading to a state of tension. Sir George Beaumont knew his father, when he studied at Eton at an early age, and he found Cozens in Rome in March of 1783, quite unwell. It was Beaumont who eventually was to be responsible for Cozens being committed to the care of Thomas Monro. Certainly once back in England, Cozens seems to have been looking for funds, and had Greenwood sell thirty views of Italy and Switzerland between 1787 -88.

There are several elements that need to be considered, but the most important is to understand to what extent Monro was responsible for the development of J.M.W. Turner and Thomas Girtin, when he eventually called on them to copy some of the artist's drawings. Cozens brought with him many drawings, and was still capable of reproducing these. Monro endeavoured to have Cozens make outline sketches, whilst he could do this, which were then coloured in by Girtin and Turner. The artist's work seemed to have had a profound impact on the doctor, who became determined to save as much as he could of Cozen's work by copying what was available, and to have him continue to produce the outlines for as long as he was capable. On 27th February, 1794, Farington wrote in his diary that "Cousins is now confined under the care of Dr. Monro, who has no expectation of his recovery, as it is a total deprivation of nervous faculty"[i] Like Cozens, Monro was well aware of the literature of his time, and certainly the moods and atmospheric effects found in the later works of Cozens, with low horizons and soft, misty English light, painted perhaps to create 'sublime effects' fitted well with the work of Wordsworth.[2] Constable we learn from his biographer Leslie, praised his work by saying "Cozens is all poetry. Leslie also wrote: 'So modest and unobtrusive are the beauties of his drawings that you might pass them without notice. He never says – look at this or that. He trusts implicitly to your own taste and feeling. His works are full of half-concealed beauties, such as nature herself shows, (figures stealing out of the landscape being as it were a part of it), but coyly, and there are often the most fleeting appearances of light. An eye equally adapted to the grandeur, the elegance and the simplicity of Nature, but he loved best not her most gorgeous language, but her gentlest – her most silent eloquence.'3

Monro happened to come on the scene, as his great grandson wrote in 1922, at a very critical moment. Not only could he afford to be a considerable collector and patron of art, but was by natural gifts himself no mean artist.4 Roget writes that the doctor himself "was no mean executant, being closer to Gainsborough's style of sketching, which has been proved since his sketches were sold to connoisseurs in the sale room over and over again as Gainsborough's work.5 Laurence Binyon was to write of Monro that he was only thirty three when he moved to Adelphi Terrace. 'He was an amateur of much taste and talent. I have seen a number of his drawings, and they entirely bear out the tradition that his landscapes comes nearer to Gainsborough than any of that master's numerous and often very skilful imitators.'6 When the doctor moved to Adelphi Terrace, Turner and Girtin were on the verge of manhood, and the proficiency of each had already been recognised. Turner was already a student at the Royal Academy, whilst Girtin seems to have met Monro either through Lord Essex, or whilst he was in prison. Again Binyon describes the day when Lord Essex paid a visit to the Fleet and found the walls of Girtin's room covered with 'such vigorous and graceful sketches that he was enchanted, paid the necessary sum to release him from the apprenticeship, and became his firm friend and constant patron.'7 Girtin had been apprenticed to Edward Dayes, a topographical draughtsman, who managed a meagre living making sketches and watercolours of picturesque sites and historical monuments. Many of these were engraved and circulated in publications geared to the tourist and antiquarian markets. Although never a member of the Royal Academy he showed landscapes and the occasional portrait there throughout the 1790's. It seems that Dayes, frustrated in his own art, was dismayed at the growing success of his young student Thomas Girtin, who had achieved before the age of twenty-five what Dayes had failed to gain at forty, critical acclaim and numerous commissions from various members of Society. Girtin did not serve the full term of his contract, and apparently Dayes had Girtin jailed for breach of contract. Meanwhile Dayes seems never to have forgiven his pupil this stroke of good fortune. Girtin found a new employer in John Raphael Smith., following his release from Bridewell.

Girtin took lessons in drawing initially from a Mr. Fisher of Aldersgate Street, before becoming an apprentice to Edward Dayes. During Girtin's imprisonment for having broken his articles with Dayes, following an argument because he was bored at being kept to colouring prints, the story of his having decorated the walls of his prison cell seem to have gone down in history with his family, as well as the descendants of Dr. Monro. However, it is doubtful that Girtin was ever in Fleet prison, which was reserved for the worst debtors, but probably more likely that he was at Bridewell, a City prison, where City apprentices would have been sent. The family credit Monro, who was then deputy-physician at Bridewell, so became aware of the young artist's skills, and came to the rescue, or more likely drew the attention of his friend Lord Essex, to the skills of the young prisoner.8 He must have had his attention drawn to the young man who was decorating the walls of his cell.

There is little doubt that it was at Raphael Smith's that Girtin and Turner came together; Girtin being of an open and vivacious nature, whilst Turner was silent, inscrutable and quite difficult. They were close comrades, if not close friends, united in their enthusiasm for their studies, as Binyon points out. It was here Girtin met Peter De Wint (1784-1849), also to become an evening student of Dr. Monro, whose style was strongly influenced by Girtin, and helped by John Varley, whom he also met at Monro's academy. Even before Monro moved to Adelphi Terrace, he and Lord Essex were friends, and Essex took Girtin to his country house Cassiobury, at Bushey. This was some years before the Monro family moved to Bushey, from where they were constantly in touch with Essex, and dined in each others' houses, often with members of their house parties. There seems plenty of evidence that it was through friendship that these two artistic men were able to come to the aid of Girtin. By November, 1795, Dr. Monro is recorded by Farington as having called on him, because "he wishes to obtain admission to the Royal Academy for Girtin, a young man of 20 years of age, as a student. I told him I would undertake to obtain it if he is sufficiently advanced in drawing the human figure." Farington also recorded that the doctor then proceeded to buy an outlined and washed drawing of Wenlock Abbey from Farington, showing again his constant interest in collecting drawings.9 Turner meanwhile, was already a member of the Academy Schools, having joined in 1789, and first exhibited there in 1791, whilst Girtin never did become a member or student of the Royal Academy, although exhibiting some of his work there.

Dr. Steers described to Farington the Monro Academy, or evening meetings of the young men who met there. Farington recorded "It was in or about the year 1793 that Dr. Thomas Monro, then 34 years of age, removed from Bedford Square, where he had previously resided, to No. 8 Adelphi Terrace, which row of houses had been built about 20 years before by the brothers Adam, and then over-hung the Thames, as it now overhangs the river embankment.

His house was filled with pictures and drawings, many by Gainsborough, hanging on the walls and he allowed them to be freely copied by young artists."10 This event was also recorded by his son, Edward Thomas, in his Summary of My Life, written presumably in his later years. Pye, the engraver, writes that the first mention of Thomas Monro's journal was in 1793, but without the journal other references have become quite important in trying to understand just when Monro began to encourage artists to make use of his house. There was a lack of formal training for aspiring artists when in 1794 an informal group of young artists began to meet regularly at the Adelphi Terrace home of Dr. Monro to colour drawings and outlines.

By 1797, we learn from Farington, who wrote in his diary in November, "Hoppners I dined at. Turner and Girtin told us they had been employed by Dr. Monro 3 years, to draw at his house in the evenings. They went at 6 and stayed till ten. Girtin drew in outlines and Turner washed in the effects. They were chiefly employed in copying the outlines of unfinished drawings of Cozens etc. of which copies they made finished drawings. Dr. Monro allowed Turner 3s.6d. per night. Girtin did not say what he had. Turner afterwards told me that Dr. Monro had been a material friend to him, as well as to Girtin, (Turner) is a son of a Turner who lived in St. Martin's Le Grand. Girtin told us he had been on a tour through North Wales with a young man from Norwich of the name of Moss – Girtin had no money- so Moss advanced him £20, & afterwards £5 more – all of which he expended as he bore half the expenses.11 Binyon mentions that "De Wint, Cotman, Hunt and Varley and others, were invited to spend the evening and copy from the doctor's pictures. They received half a crown apiece for their drawings, and an oyster supper." 12 It is said that Monro got Girtin to make outlines for Turner

27

to tint, which reminds one of Girtin's earlier rebellion at the monotony of colouring prints, though now we hear Girtin complained that he had not an equal opportunity for learning to paint! In the Catalogue of Monro's sale, which took place in 1833, there were listed six copies by Girtin from Cozens, besides a drawing 'in the manner of Barrett', and a copy from Hearne. Turner, most assiduous of copyists in his youth, seems to have preferred Cozens as a model, to any other artist. Cozens would doubtless interest Girtin as being the first English master of water-colours, and no doubt he could learn much from him, but we do not hear of any expressed admiration for Cozens, such as Turner emphatically acknowledged. Meanwhile Turner attended the sale of Monro's effects, in order to buy back much of his early work. He is recorded to have said to Dr. Burney, well known at the time as a musical patron, who attended the sale: "Well, perhaps they are not so bad, for half-a-crown and one's oysters."

The effect of the work of Cozens, discovered by Turner through his association with the Monro Academy, caused him to try and emulate what he saw. In 1794, when he was nineteen, he was already making competent copies after engravings, studying the drawings and making meticulous topographical watercolours. Cozens technique was to build up tones in watercolour by means of layers of carefully placed small brush strokes, so that the whole structure of the scene was expressed in terms of mass rather than outline, along with a great sensitivity to atmosphere. Turner was to give a clear imitation of the new sense of drama that J.R. Cozens was to infuse into English art. C.R. Leslie tells us that Cozens exhibited only once at the Royal Academy, in 1776, with a painting in oils entitled: *A Landscape with Hannibal on his March over the Alps, showing his army the fertile plains of Italy.* This wrote Leslie, 'I have heard, was an oil picture, and so fine that

Turner spoke of it as a work from which he learned more than from anything he had seen.'13/14 Turner in 1830 returned to the image with his Palestrina. By 1794 it is known that Turner was working also on engravings for the Copper Plate Magazine, sometime's referred to as Walker's Magazine, where he worked with Girtin. Girtin produced a View of Windsor in May of 1792, when he was only seventeen, and Turner's name appears on a View of Rochester, 1794. 15 Edward Dayes also worked at one time for Walker's Magazine, tinting over Indian ink with accuracy and skill, and excelling in architectural subjects. Girtin soon mastered Dayes's watercolour style, shadowed in grey and blue, and washed over with faded over colours of pink, yellow-green and sandy-orange on his fashionable antique ruins, so much in vogue at this time. As a result of this work in copying, Girtin early became a skilled architectural draughtsman. Turner although professing to be closely influenced by J.R. Cozens, never set out to imitate his style, but using his ideas seemingly absorbed them into his own, whilst using streaks of light to increase the dramatic effects in his landscapes. From Hearne he may have acquired his formula for trees with solid diagonal short lines.16

Monro, it is said by his descendants, knew Turner's home background intimately, being called in from time to time to treat Turner's mother, who had what were described as 'manic rages'. He apparently patronised the skills of Turner's father as a barber. He is said to have bought the son's drawings from the barber in Maiden Lane, who was justly proud of his son's achievements. Roget recorded this fact as coming from the engraver John Pye. Roget also wrote that Pye declared that in Dr. Monro's opinion the great painter was "blunt, craise, vulgar and sly", but in spite of all this Turner did say that Monro had been a material friend to him.17 Turner's home life was not of a kind to which he could easily expose his friends. He became a loner, with a mother who had periods of manic rage, culminating in her confinement in the Bethlem Hospital, coming under the care of Dr. Monro. She was eventually moved to Monro's private nursing home at Brook House. Turner seems to have trained briefly under various masters, including Sandby's school in St. Martin's Lane, where he worked under Thomas Hardwick in training as an architect. It was the artist J.F. Rigaud who eventually introduced him to the Academy Schools in 1789. Turner's friendship with Girtin was from working with him, since there was also a connection with the two artists in those early years, both working for John Raphael Smith, who was a skilful mezzotinter, producing prints from the paintings of beauties by Reynolds, Gainsborough and Romney. Smith also drew and painted, dealt in prints, and published them at this place in King Street, close to Maiden Lane, where Turner lived at No. 26. ((Girtin's sketchbook of 1800 has a pen-and-ink sketch, J.R. Smith waiting for the Mail coach.) Girtin may have coloured prints for Smith as part of his work under Dayes. We are told that he disposed of his own drawings through Jack Harris, frame-maker and boon-companion of Smith. All these facts help towards understanding how it was that when Monro was looking for artists capable of reproducing the work of Cozens, once he had been entrusted to his care he called on two young men who were already well known to him, and rapidly becoming artists of note in their own right.

Edward Dayes in his book affords some clue as to the relations of the professional draughtsmen, the engravers and the amateurs, and how in their combined undertakings they produced a golden age of dilettantism. Sir George Beaumont was perhaps the leader, with his own talent for landscape painting, and his concern and interest in the work of so many artists of his day, including Cozens. Beaumont owned a volume of Sketches in Italy amongst his collections at Coleorton, made by J.R. Cozens when he went to Italy in 1776 with Richard Payne Knight, who was his sponsor. For Beaumont art was an important escape from his political activities. Not only did he build his own gallery in anticipation of his collection, but he took painting seriously himself, and showed his preference for watercolour landscapes. With Richard Payne Knight and his friends he found time to help raise a subscription to help care for Cozens. He and Monro were friends, which is how Beaumont came to hear of promising artists, and he certainly met Girtin at Monro's house. Both Girtin and later Constable, were invited to Coleorton to study Beaumont's collection of paintings, especially his watercolours, and both artists were later to acknowledge the importance of this opportunity on their future work. Another description mentions Redgrave's Dictionary of Artists where 'more than one instance is recorded of artists who owed their chance and their training to him (Thos. Monro) And of one or two it is related that when they came to die they still had a friend,' and were 'Buried in Bushey Churchyard at the expense of their old friend, Thomas Monro. He had done all he could to help them, put them in the way of pursuing their art: cared for them in their sickness and took upon himself the expense of their burial. Such a record of faithful friendship is a record supremely worth having.'[18] Henry Edridge was certainly buried in Bushey Churchyard, with a tombstone bearing a carved artists' palette and brushes, organised after his death in 1821 by his old friend Monro.

The sentimental and emotional portion of Highland generosity and kindness may have been instrumental in Thomas Monro initially agreeing to take J.R. Cozens into his care, and confine him to one of his homes, where he personally took care of him. How much Monro knew of Cozens' work before he had an incurable breakdown is not known. Cozens appears to have appealed emotionally to Monro's artistic sense. Roget reports that it was 'as a physician, skilled in like cases, that he (Monro) was able to perform this kind service to this afflicted artist. Receiving little as a gratuity he treated him with the greatest care and tenderness until his death.'[19] Sir George Beaumont may also have suggested this, since he was after this responsible for encouraging the Royal Academy and other friends to contribute to his upkeep. This is made clear by Joseph Farington in numerous entries in his diary. In July of 1796, he reports that he 'called on Yenn for money due to Cozens and J. Wilson, but Richards pays this day the Academy Charity.'[20] This would seem to indicate that there was a Charity or Pension Fund set up so that some artists might receive an allowance, and we learn from the Farington diary that on June 20th, 1795, Richards had informed him 'that he paid Mr. Roberts, Brother-in-law to poor Cozens, ten guineas last year on the Academy account.' In June of that same year Lady Beaumont had written to Farington telling him that West (Benjamin) had subscribed 3 guineas towards the maintenance of poor Cozens, at a guinea annually. She desired Farington, by West's direction to address a letter to the Council to recommend Cozens as an object of charity. However, it was again necessary to raise funds in 1797, as Farington has two entries in his diary for May: 'Sir George Beaumont called on and got his signature as a voucher for the unhappy situation of Cozens.' May 13: 'Mr Knight called on and got his signature to the voucher for Cozens. Roberts called on me; gave him the statement signed by Sir George Beaumont and Mr. Knight, also a form of circular letter which they had approved.'[21] This would suggest that members of the R.A. were being appealed to for further funds. By July 15th, 1797, there is another entry of interest, when Farington wrote that 'Roberts called – I told him I had obtained 4 guineas for Mrs. Cozens. He said they were not married – she is a Booksellers daughter. They had a daughter Sophia, who was apparently paid an allowance by the Academy Fund until she died in 1845. Roberts was married to J.R. Cozens's sister Julia. Cozens died in 1797, at Northampton House on St. John Street, Smithfield, an establishment of Monro's, one of several private houses used for the insane coming under the doctor's care, managed by a Mr. Holmes. He was kept for a guinea a week, and treated by Monro free of charge. He was buried in St. James' Church, Clerkenwell.

His great-grandson was to write of Thomas Monro as being a kindly, hospitable man, who loved beauty for its own sake, and cared not a jot whether the friends and disciples with whom he surrounded himself were well or humbly born, so long as they too could show a love for beauty and pursue art with reverence and determination. At first the young men who came to learn were set to copy drawings and prints chosen from Thomas Monro's collection, to which he was always adding. Here they were taught to draw in outlines, and how to wash in tints of colour. Turner copied not only the drawings by J.R. Cozens, but also those by Paul Sandby and Thomas Hearne. Roget describes that: 'Dr. Monro's patronage of young artists was not confined to giving them access to his pictures and portfolios, and letting them make copies, but assisting them with his own judicious advice. He had a pleasant way of bringing them together, on a system which combined the benefit of this kind of study with mutual instruction, and with a small pecuniary profit to them at the same time.'22 We also learn that from six to ten on winter evenings, he encouraged young men to make a studio of his house. There they put their sketches into pictorial shape under doctor's eye, and gave them their supper and half-a-crown apiece for their work. Double desks were constructed, facing one another, so that one candle, and very likely one water-pot or one ink-pot, would serve for two students sitting face to face. His grandson wrote that 'in the early days Turner and Girtin and others came as boys. But as the years went on we find the names of Cotman, John and Cornelius Varley, W.H. Hunt, John Linnell, Copley Fielding, Peter de Wint, and Joshua Cristall, and old Tom Hearne, who came not to learn but to assist in the teaching, as did Henry Edridge, who was a great friend and constant visitor. John Varley introduced Copley Fielding. Varley had two sisters; one was married to Fielding and the other to John Linnell. To add to this description William Foxley Norris, his great grandson, wrote: 'I have a small and very fine water-colour of a mill by Thomas Hearne (signed) and my mother told me that when this was given to her by her father she was told to prize it because "Mr. Turner", then rising to great fame, had had to copy it over and over again as a boy till he got in every detail, to his kindly patron's satisfaction. Later these boys, for some were little more – were allowed to do original sketches out of the window, and I have one in sepia of a bridge with barges and the Shot Tower. Whether this is by Turner or Girtin it is difficult to say, but there is very little doubt that it is by one or the other.' He goes on to say 'Incidentally in return for the half-crown and supper, he (Monro) kept their sketches: and if they had not nearly all been sold at his death in 1833, when Turner was of course still alive, and both his and Girtin's work could be had for quite a small price, the occasional half-crown might have proved a wonderful investment for the family.' He continues: "I have in my possession an old battered portfolio containing a number of scraps, odds and ends of paper, bits of letters, programmes, invitations, bills. On the backs of these, or wherever there happened to be a piece of clean paper, are sketches – some in ink, some in pencil – of faces, heads, figures. Many of them can be readily identified. Half a dozen were exhibited at South Kensington, and have been reproduced. They are portraits of Turner, Girtin, Edridge, Laporte, Thomas Hearne, Lord Essex, Thomas Monro, Henry Monro, Mrs. Thomas Monro, Miss Monro and others. One or two are caricatures. But most of them slight as they are, are serious portrait studies and sketches. Who did any one of these particular drawings we do not know for certain, but no doubt they were done by various members of the group of young artists who used to meet at the Doctor's house sketching one another at odd moments."23

Foxley Norris also left a good description of the method in fashion when Monro began his school in 1794. "When colour was introduced, there is no doubt that the well-known old method of making a complete drawing in Payne's grey, then adding local colour on top of the grey wash was used. This is an excellent method of getting tone and quality without losing transparency or sacrificing the essential character of water-colour work. But this is an old story. It has been described again and again. It is to be found in the work of very many of the afterwards eminent men who worked with the doctor, and it is elaborated in one or two books of the period published to help beginners, notably one by W.H. Pyne, published by Ackerman in 1812, entitled *Rudiments of Landscape* When colour was introduced, there is no doubt that the well-known old method of making a complete drawing in Payne's grey, and then adding local colour on the top of the grey wash, was used. This is an excellent method of getting tone and quality without losing transparency or sacrificing the essential character *Drawing in a series of Easy Examples.* In this book (of which I have a copy) the process is clearly described and illustrated. First there is the 'perspective outline' which is really a free drawing on the lines of the perspective, then the 'first shadows' in grey, then the 'finished effect' still in grey; and then the local colour is added on top of the grey foundation.'24

Cozens retained monochromatic underpainting used by the earliest exponents of watercolour, and as a legacy from the oil technique. Girtin experimented with light brown paper bought from a special shop in Charing Cross, which he folded in the middle. There were several in the collection of Lord Harewood. His richness of colour on cartridge paper, was less laborious than executing it on white paper. He usually finished his compositions on the spot, after much study and proportionate manual dexterity. Girtin early formed his own style of shorthand, with a hooked and dotted line, showing an instinctive sense of composition, encouraged by Thomas Hearne. Turner not only used body colour, mixing his colours with white, but also partially wiped out his colour with rags and sponges, or more often the balls of bread his kept in his pocket. He often scratched the surface with a knife, or even his thumbnail – kept long for the purpose, to get extra lights. Farington reported that "Turner has no settled process but drives the colours about until He has expressed the idea in his mind." 25 Hawkesworth Fawkes of Farnley in Yorkshire described his methods while the artist was staying with him, as Turner sketched before lunch. "The paper was soaked, blistered, daubed, rubbed and scratched with the thumbnail until at length beauty and order broke from chaos." The sea always fascinated Turner, not just the light, air and water, but men and ships too. Turner, who would sketch a landscape for twenty five guineas for a magazine printer almost to the end of his life, could always turn out an "early" water colour, - 'all tinted steam', as Constable referred to them, for his own pleasure.

From the sale that took place at Christies in 1833 after

36

Monro's death, it was seen that Monro possessed many books of drawings by Turner and Girtin, and others by the 'Monro School'26. Two lots were bought by Turner and five by his agent Thomas Griffith, a majority of which were in a mixture of India ink and blue wash. A great number of drawings were attributed to Turner. It remains difficult for scholars to attribute these to any particular artist, although many have been reattributed to Girtin, who was certainly responsible in 1794 and 1795 for much of the outline work. Farington used the word 'traced' in his diary of December 30, 1794, and evidence seems to point to Girtin as having done just that with the outlines of some of the drawings by J.R. Cozens. It is almost certain, but never proved, that when Cozens came under the care of Monro he had drawings in his possession, several made for his patron William Beckford, or his own copies of these, and others of English scenes from 1784. Cozens continued to draw from memory, 'so long as he was capable' we are given to understand.27 To further complicate authenticity, not only were Turner and Girtin close in style in those years, but there is still some uncertainty as to who were the students that made up the Monro School at that time. Probably Thomas Underwood (1772-1835) was also involved, and he knew Girtin well. With Girtin he helped copy sketches by James Moore (1762-1799) for Monro. Moore was Girtin's employer and travelling companion in 1795 and 1797 when they travelled north. Moore was described by C.F. Bell as being an amateur, whose means were derived from a business as a wholesale linen draper in Cheapside, who was an ambitious but not very accomplished draughtsman. Girtin helped him form his early style, first travelling with him to Scotland in 1795. Thomas Girtin, the artist's grandson wrote: "Good evidence of pre-1794 copying is in the existence of a watercolour by T.R. Underwood, in the Girtin collection. This is signed and dated October, 1793, and is an adaptation of the aquatint of Battle Abbey, or perhaps a Dayes' drawing for it, published in Monastic Remains, July 1, 1791. This again was from a sketch by Moore, who visited Battle on July 10, 1790. The Underwood drawing came direct from the Monro collection, not in card form, unlike many of the card drawings signed by Moore and Dayes, and finished in 1792, which went to the engravers. (Landseer for Forsyth's Beauties of Scotland and Walker for the Copper Plate Magazine). I suspect that Underwood's drawing of the Eleanor Cross at Waltham Abbey (V&A 407-1885) has the same provenance. This is dated January 1793, and was aquatinted by Parkyns as from a sketch by J.C. Barrow after Moore. Barrow dressed up Moore's sketches for Parkyns." 28

On the fifth day of Monro's sale, the Dayes' drawings were sold under Numbers 36-54. The grandson of Girtin the artist wrote: "The first five lots, 36-40, contained 101 drawings – coloured sketches of Antiquities and Buildings. The thought is irresistible that these were the main sources from which the 'drawings on card' were copied". No mention of pencil drawings by Dayes is made under his name in the Monro sale catalogue, but it is possible that they may have lain concealed among a number of miscellaneous sketches in the catalogue. At any rate Turner acquired a number of them. It is likely that the majority of the subjects originally sketched by Moore, dressed up by Dayes and used by Perkyns for his acquatints in *Monastic Remains and Ancient Castles* were probably acquired by Monro from Dayes himself. Girtin's grandson points out that Monro consigned forty of them to a Turner group, though others were given to the family. With the cachet of Monro and the name of Turner all these cards have descended as by Turner and will doubtless continue to do so unless more contemporary evidence is found. In some cases several copies may have been made since the copying was continued, and even carried out by Monro's sons Alexander and John until the break up of the collection. Again from work that was in the Turner Bequest, and from examples in the British Museum collections, Wilton mentions that "it seems Turner and Girtin were employed in 1797 in a long series of small watercolours, perhaps in a projected topographical work. probably for Dr. Monro, since he owned several such books."29 *Conniston Falls, Middleton Vale, Yorks* was a small picture, by Turner, and may have been one of these. Turner copied this in oils to show at the R.A. in 1798. Andrew Wilton writes further of the drawings by James Moore FSA in his new edition of his book *Monastic Remains & Ancient Castles in England and Wales -1812* edition in two volumes, saying, "several conform to subjects in the Turner Bequest quite likely to have been by Girtin. These were working drawings, and although the original inspiration may have come from Dayes – derived from his drawings, it seems they may have come from Thomas Monro originally, and were amongst drawings at his sale done by Girtin."

In November, 1806, the diary of Edward Thomas Monro tells us that Linnell, Hunt and Turner came to draw, indicating that the facilities offered to these artists by Dr. Monro were still available to them. It was at this time that J.M.W. Turner was about to publish his *Liber Studiorum,* so he may well have been working on his engravings. He may have made use of the printing press, which Tom records in his diary that he had to clean, so we know Dr. Monro had one at Adelphi Terrace. Although his first works were not published until 1809, Turner continued working on these until 1819, with seventy-one of his intended one hundred prints appearing. The venture failed through lack of support, and Turner's efforts to run the advertising and publishing all on his own. The *Liber* drawings were monochrome, following the style used by Claude, but also something that Dr. Monro had encouraged his pupils to use in colouring in their outlines. Turner generally worked from coloured drawings, which had the advantage of being able to be sold afterwards. Engravers also preferred to work from coloured drawings, a skill that Turner and Girtin had mastered between them when working initially for Raphael Smith in Covent Garden.

Tom recorded in his diary of January 13th, 1807, that Daniell, Farington, Hearne, Edridge and Alexander dined. These gentlemen were all part of Monro's inner circle and were frequent visitors to the Adelphi Terrace house drawing evenings, with the exception of Joseph Farington. They visited the Monro's country house at Bushey quite frequently, as we know from a description by Farington in his diary. Certainly Edridge enhanced the success of the evenings, since he played and sang well, according to Monro's great-grandson. Moreover, says Foxley Norris, he had a knack of getting likeness with remarkable facility in his rapid pencil sketches. They were done, it is said, very quickly and easily. There are several of the family of George lll in the Royal Collection. Redgrave speaks of Edridge as one of the greatest masters of the period both in pure English water-colour, and in pencil drawing. We also know from the diaries kept by Tom, that the two Hoppners, father and son, were frequently in and out, and that William Alexander, with his precise skill in drawing, was also a frequent visitor. Tom writes about supper upstairs for his mother and Sally, his sister, on several occasions. Foxley Norris writes that "my great-grandmother was inclined from time to time to retire into her shell, and to have dinner upstairs, and my great aunt Sally occasionally complained of the invasion of the house by what would no doubt today be described as Bohemians. But my genial great-grandfather cared for none of these things. Whether he had the slightest notion of the height of fame to which some of his pupils were going to attain, we do not know, but they wanted to learn and they showed ability, and they were growing proficient in the new art of water-colour, and that was enough for him."30

In a letter dated 7th March, 1900. John Linnell wrote about his father's diary, and in another dated 28th March, quotes from this saying:
"Very often William (Hunt) and I went to draw for 2 hours at Dr. Monro's after the Academy. Dr. Monro had a large collection of the early drawings of Girtin and Turner, both of whom he had been in the habit of taking out to draw from nature for him, and these drawings, with compositions in charcoal by Gainsborough, of which the doctor had a great number. William Hunt and I copied for the Doctor, who paid us one shilling and sixpence the hour. We sometimes had some supper also. Some of these copies were afterwards, I have no doubt, sold for the originals again."

This is yet another indication that the school lasted for several years, having begun in 1794, although Linnell does not mention the attendance of Monro's friends, whose input on the students was so important. It is difficult to understand which of the many artists who frequented Adelphi Terrace, and Bushey, did so at the invitation of Thomas Monro directly, or who might have been friends with his son Henry, who joined the Academy Schools in 1806, and immediately became very proficient. A short sketch of Henry's career has a place in Redgrave's Dictionary, and there is no doubt that had Henry lived he would have achieved very great things, but he died in 1814, when still in his twenty third year. Henry had a studio of his own, Foxley Norris tells us, at the top of the house, and was for a brief period the centre of a considerable group of young artists, quite distinct from his father's gatherings at Adelphi Terrace. Eventually he was to move to live above a picture framer called Vinson, in Covent Garden. From time to time Henry and his friends were present at the Adelphi gatherings, as is evidenced from one or two entries in the diaries, and from indications in the little collection of sketches mentioned by Monro's great grandson. Meanwhile the period of Monro's life could be said to correspond to the rise and establishment of watercolour painting in England as a serious branch of art. The Romantic, epitomised by J.R. Cozens, and the more purely topographical, exemplified by Edward Dayes and Thomas Hearne, moved closer together, and it was here that Monro played such a key role. Monro encouraged a younger generation of artists, headed by Turner and Girtin, to seek the "poetry" of Cozens, and to observe directly from Nature, as he took many of his students to Fetcham, his first country house near Guildford, to sketch and draw outside. There is no doubt that the standard and ideals which he insisted upon had much to do with building the unrivalled position which the English school of watercolours attained. Taste also played an enormous part in what Monro was teaching to his young artist friends, coupled with knowledge. To Turner and Girtin, and to the other young artists who met at the Adelphi Terrace house on a winter evening, it must have been of inestimable benefit to come in contact with a cultured mind, well versed in the arts, which cannot be taken to have been in the same league as the drawing masters and other instructors the students met in the production of pictures. He provided an alternative at just the moment when painting in watercolour was being encouraged. Monro criticised and helped these men, as did his artistic friends Herne and Henry Edridge, and the Doctor himself must have received satisfaction from doing this, for it was in a way the fulfilment of his life's purpose. Thwarted by being deflected from a career in the arts by the necessity, both self-imposed and demanded of him, to succeed his father as Medical Superintendent of Bedlam, Monro moved close to the artistic world, choosing his friends from within that circle. Turner's imagination, coupled with diffidence, and his unconventional approach to painting, might easily have brought depression as well as frustration, to which he was already no stranger, without the sympathetic appreciation and encouragement given by the Doctor. Monro saw what was in the young man, which from time to time needed bringing out. Lastly we hear from his great grandson; "The account of the Sale that took place at his (Monro's) death, shows that he had what was then a very remarkable collection both of drawings and prints by recognised masters. The fact that this collection was in his possession had a great deal to do with the help he was able to give to young artists. It included a very considerable number of landscape sketches by Gainsborough, as well as that artist's camera obscura, with ten subjects of landscapes, seapieces and moonlight." In April, 1801, Farington dined with Monro and looked at a portfolio of eighty drawings Monro had just purchased from Miss Gainsborough for 180 guineas. Foxley Norris continues: "then there were large numbers of drawings by Cozens and T. Hearne and Dayes, and by Wilson and Paul Sandby. Canaletto, Rembrandt, Ostade, Paul Potter, Vandervelde, Kobel, Mompart, Boucher were also represented. There were sketches of Italian buildings by Claude, and a landscape in pen and ink by Titian. In addition there were many drawings and paintings by lesser men as well as very large numbers of print of various kinds. All this wealth of material was placed at the disposal of the artists who were fortunate enough to study under his roof."31

On March 5th, 1810, Farington mentioned that "Dr. Monro has had an offer made to him which has caused him to reckon up what his collection of drawings cost him, and he finds it amounts to about £3,000. Drawings by Hearne form a considerable part of them and cost him about £800." We also know from Farington that in addition Monro paid Laporte £600 for drawings. When Monro died he gave instructions in his will for his collections to be sold, except those drawn by himself, and by his sons Henry, John and Alexander. Many of these are still in the collections of descendants of his family. The sale at Christies, starting on June 26, 1833, took five days and according to the Catalogue, Appendix ll (British Museum) consisted of works by Loutherbourg, Bartolozze, Rooker, Reinagle, Barret, John Varley, de Wint and Hunt, in addition to those mentioned by his grandson. Also Neale, Alexander, Havell, Munn, Bonnington and Wheatley were represented. His father, John Monro, it has been recorded, held "conversaziones", when famous artists gathered in the evenings at the Monro household in Bedford Square, where Thomas lived before he moved to Adelphi Terrace. This may have been an influence behind the idea held by Thomas to hold evening meetings at his house to encourage young artists. The collections owned by Dr. John Monro were also considerable, being sold by Mr. Greenwood of Piccadilly, beginning on 30th April, 1792, and taking six days to complete. Few seem to have been inherited by his son, who became a collector in his own right.

1. Garlic. Kenneth, editor The Diaries of Joseph Farington Vol 111
2. Sloan, Kim Alexander & John Robert Cozens, Art Gallery of Ontario Cat. 1986 pl6
3. Leslie, C.R. Memoirs of the Life of John Constable 1845
4. Harford, G. A Short History of Bushey Artists 1769-1969 - quote from Foxley Norris
5. Roget, J. History of the Old Water-Colour Society Vol 1 p77-99
6. Binyon, Laurence Thomas Girtin Seeley & Co. Ltd. London 1900 pi 3
7. Ibid p 12
8. Lindsay, Jack Turner see footnote p294 Granada Edition. If Girtin went to jail it would have been Tothill Fields unlikely. Monro was at Bridewell at the time, whilst Tom was still at Harrow.
9. Garlic, Kenneth Diaries Vol 11 p414
10. Ibid p14
11. Ibid Vo!iUpl09
12. Binyon, Laurence p 13
13. Lindsay; Jack Turner see footnote p 294
14. Ibid p319 Lindsay quotes from 2 ed C.R. Leslie Memoirs of the Life of John Constable. Cb.6 1845 Ed.
15. Girtin's View of Windsor YFSS in the 4th No. Plate VII May 1792. Turner's work was Plate LV, 1794. Edward Dayes also worked for Walker's Magazine.
16. Lindsay. Jack Turner p 41
17. Ibid p.29
18. Redgrave S. Dictionary of Artists of the English School Bell & Son, London 1878
19. Roget, J.L. History of the Old Water-Colour Society Vol. 1 pp 77-79
20. Garlic. K. Ed. Diaries Vol B 1795-6 p 613
21. Ibid p 83 see also Walpole Soc. Vol.XXV11 - 193/39 p 89 Sketchbook of Th. Girtin
22. Roget J.L. History of the Old Water-Colour Soc. Vol. 1 pp 77-79
23. Harford, Geoffrey A Short History of Bushey Artists 1769-1969. Quotes are taken from an article written by the Very Rev. W. Foxley Norris D.D. Dean of York (great grandson of Th. Monro) in 1922 for the Old Water-Colour Society
24. Ibid
25. Garlic, K Diaries 1978 Vol 11 pl289 Nov. 1799
26. Girtin Archive at the British Museum on Monro (press mark

cc. 167.b.26 27)

27. Wilton, Andrew Turner Studies - His Art and Epoch 1775-J881 Vol 4 No.2 p8 1984 in 1901 a series of Monro School drawings from Turners studio were re-attributed to Thomas Girtin (TB CCCLXXX111 and CCCLXX1V - also XXV and X

28. Foxley-Norris A Short History of Bushey Artists. No page nos.

29. From the collection of Mrs. Coode's letters at the British Museum

30. Foxley Norris - from the Harford A Short History of Bushey Artists

31. Library of Fine Arts - iii 310

CHAPTER 3 – FAMILY LIFE

Whilst still at Oxford, pursuing his medical studies, Thomas wrote to his Oxford friend Elborough Woodcock. Thomas's letter is strangely stilted as from one young man to another, on a subject which might have led him to express his emotions frankly to a close friend. After a dissertation concerning his reserve and secrecy in the matter of Elborough's sister Hannah, Thomas writes:

> "You may remember our journey from Bath in the Spring was not enlivened by any efforts of sociality on my part, my spirits were not of the most exhilarating kind. I do not recollect that I assisted you with any striking remark, the pleasantry of which alleviated the length of the journey in any shape. On the contrary I was uncommonly silent and my mind was absorbed in contemplation. Of what? Of something I hardly knew myself at the time, but intermediate scenes have brought conviction to my senses - of her whom I had left behind who has been my constant companion of my most serious thoughts ever since - Whose image never can be effaced from my memory. In short I feel the sincerest, the greatest affection for your sister Hannah and have it in my power to say that I am honoured with an equal share of her esteem. - If I am to blame, you must answer it – you were the first tho' innocent cause of bringing us together, and of enabling me to perceive those amiable qualities in her which have won my heart beyond a possibility of redemption. To say anything further on the ardour of my passion would be indelicate and foreign to my purpose. I am making a declaration to a man who knows what the impulse of his passions can excite, and, I hope, who will make allowance (if so it should appear) in this pursuit - You are thoroughly acquainted with my principles and I am not conscious

of ever having concealed a thought from you upon any subject. I have seriously consulted with my family upon the affair, and have met with the most gratifying marks of approbation. - My father has offered to allow me £500. per annum and the advantage of living in his house. As soon as you have fully considered what I have laid before you be so kind as to favour me with your Opinion, and believe me

Yours most sincerely, Thomas"[1]

This is a complex letter when it comes to assessing the character of a young man aged twenty nine, which shows little sense of humour to his avowed great friend, although the letter's formality may have been required by the fashion of the times. Does the underlying sense of weariness or lack of enthusiasm come from the fact that he was at the time studying for a profession for which he had not originally been intended? Perhaps his reticence was caused because he hardly dared to trust his own good fortune in an affair of the heart. There are many letters from this time. Those from the Woodcock family, written from Bath during a period when that City was the centre of fashion and culture, give no references to any of the events in the gay world around the family. So many interesting letters of the important people of that time have been published that it is intriguing to find that so many dull letters should have been kept. The letters do serve to give a picture of eighteenth century life in the less fashionable circles, and to some extent depict the rather unexciting home life of a daughter who, in due course, as Hannah Monro, would be called upon to create a home life in her turn, into the pattern of which would fit Thomas Hearne, Sir George Beaumont, Edridge, John Hoppner, Lord Essex and Joseph Farington, amongst many other known contemporary names. These were part of the intimate circle outside the immediate family, not to mention the students working in the house at

Adelphi Terrace, and later frequent visitors to Bushey, the Monro house in the country.

Before discussing the letters and marriage of Thomas, a short mention of Hannah Monro's appearance does exist in Joseph Farington's diary of 1802. Mrs. Monro "when she married", he says,"had a little squint, but it was rather agreeable. Two or three years ago owing to some cause about the eyes one of them turned in the opposite direction to what it had been before. She had been much affected by the circumstances thinking it make her appearance very singular. The Dr. wished for a drawing of her by Lawrence."[2] The last sentence reveals a rather touching tribute, or perhaps the Doctor suggested the portrait to console her for what she thought was a decline in good looks.

It must have been a supreme moment of triumph in 1787 when Thomas Monro was appointed Physician of Bethlem Hospital, acquiring a job and potentially a bride, carrying with him to the Rev. Dr. Edward Woodcock the news that he was now in a position to marry his daughter. He received the following written reply:

Sunday, August 5th, 1787 My dear Sir,

> We thank you much for your early and obliging attention to our commission, and will soon trouble you to compleat it.

> Whenever our friends at Lincoln's Inn are ready, and you and my daughter fix upon a time agreeable to you, I shall most readily accede to the union, which I trust will prove happy. In the mean time, we shall be heartily glad to see you at your convenience. We join in best respects to Dr. and Mrs. Monro: all desire to be kindly remembered to you and I remain,

Dear Sir,

Your affectionate humble servant,
Edwd. Woodcock[3]

Among this and other letters there has been preserved a
note addressed only to "Dr. Thos.Monro", signed with
young Woodcock's initials, one of Hannah's brothers. It
read:

"Dear Thos.   Wednesday (no date)

You receive herewith the great book of prints, the little
we will send tomorrow.

     Yours affectly, E.W. Temple"

The interest in this letter is that it shows that Thomas
Monro had already started collecting independently. The
bulk of his father John's collection was not sold until 1792,
taking six days to complete. Thomas seems not to have
inherited many of the works, preferring to collect himself
according to his own taste.

Eventually the announcement of the young couple's
firstborn was acknowledged by the Rev. Woodcock as
follows:

"Sunday 15 Nov. 1789

My dear Sir,

We most heartily rejoice with you upon our dear Han's
safe delivery, of the birth of your son: we were grown
impatient and the good account has essentially relieved
her mother's usual anxiety. We hope to hear that all
goes on well. My wife or I shall either of us be ready to
answer for your little boy, exactly as you may find most
convenient. I will trouble you with Mr. Hoare's book by
Mr. Allen soon, which I shall thank you to leave to be
posted up, and then call for and return it to me by
coach, not the mail, if you please. We all join in kindest
Love and Regards as due, believe me,

My dear Sir, very sincerely yours, EW"

Even the joy at the arrival of their first grandson, Edward Thomas, known as Tom, or sometimes E.T., is seen in this letter to be tempered by anxious instructions about a relatively small matter. Dr. Woodcock from his various letters seems quite a demanding man, also one who often changed his mind about affairs. His daughter appears to have suffered from the same state of mind, making it difficult for her to deal with their eventually large and wayward family. A member of the family wrote at a later date that Thomas Monro was "artistic, temperamental and dreamy and procrastinating, his wife not practical or strong-minded. He was unsuccessful of managing his own sons in his own home." Farington meanwhile wrote in 1796, "Monro is a remarkably silent man in company."[4] Perhaps he had become so because he was by the nature of his profession a listener, rather than a person who immediately stated his views. Farington continued: "He told us that his professional situation does not allow of his quitting London for several days together. He has not been four days together absent from London in the last 4 years."[5] It was at this time that Monro was involving himself with the Adelphi Terrace School, or the meeting of young students at his house, which perhaps came as a form of recreation when one considers his busy life as a doctor.

There are many letters which pass from the Rev. Woodcock regretting yet another cancelled visit from the young couple to Bath. They seemed to send frequent presents of fish, and even venison from London, but do not visit themselves. In a letter of 15th August, 1791, Woodcock wrote "my window will entice your pencil, and I have a most pleasant spare room for you." It seems all were aware of Monro's habit of taking his 'pencil' and sketchbook wherever he went.

The Monro's eldest son seems early in life to have been a diary writer, and from a 'History of Himself' we can find that he has an amazing recollection for various family events, and he also records the growth of the family. In 1791 his brother Henry was born, frequently referred to by him as 'poor Henry', perhaps on account of his early death at the age of twenty three. Henry was very artistic, and went to the Royal Academy as a student in 1807. The two brothers seem to have been devoted to one another, Henry being less reserved, full of humour, excitement, fun and sometimes the absurd, whilst Tom or E.T. was the serious doctor to be, often left with responsibilities by his mother such as putting the house in London in order before travelling to the country, or packing up the silver, and also with a developing sense of responsibility in watching out for Henry. Henry seems to have left Harrow school quite early, possibly at the age of fourteen, and was given a room at the top of the house as his studio. He soon found this inconvenient, especially as regards his "ay de camps" (boys who helped him by sitting for him, grinding colours and other odd jobs), and also his other models who were not always the sort whom "Madam" his mother cared to meet upon the stairs. He moved in 1810 to Covent Garden, above a carver and gilder named Vinson, a few years before his early death in 1814. Henry was however, a much better playmate to his three younger brothers than was the more earnest Tom. A daughter Hannah, was born in September, 1793, and the following year Sally was born, and christened in November. Sally grew up to be a family favourite with sweet and endearing ways, and was quite proficient on the piano. Theodore was born in 1796. The following year seems to have been a bad one, since "My Mother so ill as to lose the use of her limbs" is recorded, whilst little Theodore died and E.T. had the measles very badly, all recorded by Tom in his 'History of Myself'. Little Hannah, almost four years old, died of consumption, a disease that seemed fairly commonplace in those days, Another son Robert, was born in 1798, to be educated like the others at Harrow. He went like Tom to Oxford, and was eventually ordained by the Bishop of Gloucester and appointed to the Clifton Parish Church in Bristol. There were two younger sons, John was born in 1801 and Alexander the following year. They seem not to be mentioned very often in the diaries, Tom being well into his twelfth year when the youngest was born, and away at school, so it is no wonder that they were often referred to by him merely as "the little boys". Sally and Henry, both of whom recorded various family events, seldom mention them. John is referred to as a painter, whilst Alexander became a quite considerable artist. Hearne and Edridge went out sketching at Bushey and were sometimes accompanied by Alexander. John was the despair of his family when young since he had violent fits of temper, but he was a competent artist. He eloped with the housemaid, Harriet Chitty, intending to get married, but was pursued by his cousin Frederick Monro and a Major Newton, who caught up with them. However the couple later married, lived a devoted life, and John taught her to draw. There are many of his beautifully drawn sketches still in existence, with softer outlines than those of his brother Alexander. He died in 1880. We also learn from the family diaries that Alexander eloped to Gretna Green with Harriet Withy, when he was nineteen, a daughter of his father's friend. Tom was the brother who sent them money to bring them back from Scotland, and to arrange lodgings for them, although his parents did eventually give them an allowance. The Withy family, who were "very angry and distressed" according to Tom's diary, saw that they were married in church shortly after this. Sadly Harriet only lived for just over 2 years, dying 5 December 1823, 2 weeks after having given birth to a daughter, who also died. Donald survived, and Alex and his baby son lived subsequently at home at Bushey, until his father's death. He did eventually remarry, to Lucy Agnew, and had three more children. His marriage seems to have brought Alex sufficient means to have enabled him to dispense with the necessity of working or selling pictures. Alexander became an artist, but was not regarded as having the exceptional skills possessed by his late brother Henry. He and John both went to Harrow and eventually shared a studio on Hadlow Street. Alexander was to become skilled in architectural drawings, and his watercolours were much influenced by the early work of Girtin and Turner. He died in 1844. This must have been a busy family, especially when they all had to contend with their father's students frequently visiting the house once they had moved to Adelphi Terrace in 1794.

Number 8 Adelphi Terrace was in a row of houses which had warehouses underneath them and overhung the Thames. It was within an area where many artists chose to live, not within the narrow social world marked off by Pall Mall, St. James' Street, Piccadilly and Whitehall. We now consider Adelphi Terrace, beside Somerset House, and near Covent Garden, to have been the centre of the developing artistic world in London in the late eighteenth century. The Society of Arts was in the vicinity, with its Great Room or lecture theatre, also designed by Robert Adam. This was where James Barry painted a series of historical scenes on the walls, and after a labour of seven years was given the proceeds of two exhibitions held there in 1783 and 1784. It was a fashionable area, which may have tempted the Monros to move there. The houses were raised above the water level, standing over brick vaults, with the Thames being artificially embanked, all being built under an Act of Parliament in 1775. Before the formation of the Water-Colour Society in 1804, the Adelphi Academy, attached to the Society of Arts, was formed with a powerful group of drawing masters. Adelphi Terrace was a row of private houses, alongside. The main blocks of the Adelphi Terrace have been destroyed but originally the Adelphi, designed by the brothers Adam, Robert and James, was on an artificial embankment, and almost alongside Somerset House. Garrick led the way in buying his house by auction and others were soon to follow. It was a fashionable address. John Henderson, a close friend of Monro, and also an art patron, lived almost next door at No. 3 or 4, whilst their other neighbour was Mrs. Garrick, widow of the famous actor. Many houses in London at this time did not bear numbers but were distinguished by a variety of fanlights above the front door. Henderson allowed young artists to make copies of the works of older masters possessed by him, for example drawings by Canaletto and Piranesi and Melton, which Turner and Girtin certainly did. Girtin certainly copied from the Canaletto drawings, and both artists absorbed Canaletto's use of the picturesque possibilities of familiar scenes in London, with his subtle changing of the emphasis of certain architectural features, his detailed foregrounds and lack of perspective in his middle grounds. Girtin in particular began to absorb some of the dots, dashes and wavy lines that were used by Canaletto as a form of shorthand, and he was to make these very much a part of his style of drawing. Henderson kept some copies, which at his death were given to the National Collections by his son, where they could be studied by anyone wanting to discover the differences between the two young painters.

The children's early lives revolved around the house at Adelphi Terrace and the country house at Merry Hill in Bushy, Hertfordshire, which will be frequently referred to as Bushey. Before moving there, in 1809, the Monro family had initially rented a house at Fetcham, near Leatherhead in Surrey, with their first summer being spent there in 1796.Many of his friends stayed there to draw with Thomas Monro, and several of his pupils. Monro spent summers there, and his three eldest children would have remembered the house. He took his pupils there, and both Turner and Girtin drew in the vicinity. John Cotman, newly arrived from Norfolk, was certainly a guest on several occasions, mentioned by Farington as well, as having accompanied

Monro. Cotman became a student at the evening gatherings of young painters at Adelphi Terrace. . John Varley made several visits, as did Monroe's friend Hoppner, the artist, and his son Lacelles, who was a good friend of Henry Monro. Henry Edridge and Thomas Hearne were also visitors, as was Joseph Farington, who left a detailed description of his visit in 1803 in his diary. Farington travelled with Hoppner, and they visited the village of Bookham where Henry Edridge had lodgings. He learned that the house belonged to Mr. Hankey, a Banker, and that Monro "had improved it much but has doubts about keeping it after his term is expired."[6] When the move took place in 1807, it seems partly to have been due to Thomas Monro's friendship with Lord Essex whose house at Bushey, Cassiobury, contained many works of art, and was also a centre for artists to visit. Harrow school was nearby, where all five Monro boys went, so Bushey and the Monro house, Merry Hill, became a paradise for artists and for the young. The first prolonged visit by the Monros appears to have been in 1807, according to the eldest son's diary.

Because Edward Thomas, (Tom) left such a detailed diary, much is known about life at Bushey and also about the numerous visitors there, as the young Monro family played cricket, shot with bows and arrows, gardened, farmed, and sketched - in fact behaved as any normal family might. They were constantly the guests of Lord Essex at Cassiobury, a patron of the arts and especially important to the artist Thomas Girtin, since Lord Essex befriended him when he left his apprenticeship with Edward Dayes. Essex and his wife were like many other neighbours, frequently dropping in on the Monros at Bushey, where they no doubt found something to amuse or interest them. The Doctor frequently entertained Thomas Hearne, Henry Edridge, William Alexander, and Reinagle, whilst William Hunt, and Turner and Girtin were also visitors. Peter de Wint sketched there with the Doctor, in 1807 and again in 1809, when he played cricket and went to church with the family staying from 13th to 16th July. The Monro's were perpetually engaged in 'Do it Yourself', which in itself must have amused and entertained their more conventional friends. William Henry Hunt suffered from continual ill-health and we are told when he stayed at Cassiobury or Bushey, he used to be trundled about on a sort of barrow, with a hood over it, which was drawn by a man or a donkey.[7] There are no titled topographical works by either Turner or Girtin which relate to Bushey, although both artists are recorded as visiting by Tom in his diary, however there are several by Thomas Hearne, Henry Edridge, as well as Henry Hunt, and many by members of the Monro family.[8]

From a description on Monro by his great grandson a little more of his character is revealed. He wrote:

> "day after day he would drive about the lanes and farms round his country home, in a low pony chaise, with a pad of paper and charcoal or India ink, making compositions and sketches, scores of which have been preserved and are in existence. These drawings show a depth of feeling, a sense of composition, and a truth of tone, which leave no doubt as to his gifts as an artist."[9]

In his style of sketching we know he was much influenced by Gainsborough, and this acquaintance may have been made through Dr. Charlton of Bath, whose portrait Gainsborough painted, and who may possibly have been a friend of John Monro, the father of Thomas, although there is no letter or documentation to prove this. However we read in the description of him at Bushey that "so proficient did he become, that in the mass of drawings that resulted it is not always easy even for an expert to say for certain which are his and which are Gainsborough's work."[10] Gainsborough's daughter Margaret had a serious mental breakdown in 1771, from which she was never to completely recover, having lapses from time to time, and this disaster was to 'shadow Gainsborough for the rest of his life,'[11] Perhaps the artist may have consulted with John Monro, and perhaps acknowledged the favour by instructing his son Thomas, who would then have been about twelve years old. Gainsborough had first consulted Dr. Moysey, then called in Charleton and Schomberg, who cured her at that time, and there seems not to have been any mention of John Monro in an official capacity. It is not known how John LaPorte, who was tutor for a short period to Thomas, as well as being a close friend, came into the style, as he also imitated Gainsborough's way of sketching landscapes, and was no doubt a strong influence on the doctor's style.

Farington's diary tells us that following his marriage in 1789, the doctor told him that he inherited from his father an inclination for drawings. It was at the insistence of a CaptainVandeput of the Navy, that he became acquainted with LaPorte, who painted a great deal for him. He quotes that "He (Monro) has paid £5 or £6 for drawings"[12] Monro certainly knew the family, and bought Gainsborough's magic box, or camera obscura, with ten scenes, indicated by his son Tom's diary as being in 1810, from Margaret Gainsborough who lived at 63 Sloane Street. It appeared as Lot 168 on the third day of Monro's sale after his death in 1833, described as the 'camera obscura with ten subjects, landscapes, sea-pieces and moonlights, beautifully painted by Gainsborough and purchased from Miss Gainsborough shortly after the painter's death.' This was certainly in the family by January, 1811, when Tom recorded several evenings spent looking at it. For many years the widely publicised discussion of Gainsborough's painting was that which appeared in Reynold's Discourse XIV, delivered after Gainsborough's death, in 1788, where Reynolds consigned the artist to the "humble although highly successful "lower rank of art", whilst professing his preference for "genius in the lower rank of art, to feebleness and insipidity in the highest". Reynolds disliked the random and sketchy brushstrokes, although he acknowledged that "these odd scratches and marks" were taken as evidence of manner. Reynolds claimed to be impressed by the visual impact of the technique. It was the opinion of W.H. Pyne that Gainsborough's importance lay in his broadly sketched views of the English countryside, which had an impact on amateurs through his influence on the formation of the picturesque. Gainsborough provided the "designs" that "produced a love of the picturesque" among artists and amateurs, such as Dr.Thomas Monro.[13]

At this time several talented young artists were finding landscape subjects in the greater London area, such as John Linnell. Some localities were favoured more than others, largely because of patronage and accessibility, and one such place was Bushey. Dr. Monro played no small part in this as each summer he brought his family and friends to Bushey, many of them to draw, and his son's diaries give evidence of those years. He himself came and went, being a very busy man, in charge of the Bethlem Hospital; an authority on the treatment of insanity,[14] Monro also had some interest in the Brompton Hospital, in which Mr. Cox of the Foundling Hospital had a large share. Samuel Cox was Treasurer at the Foundling Hospital, and eventually Monro's eldest son, Tom Monro, had a regular job at Brompton after his marriage to Sarah Cox. The Foundling Hospital was founded by Captain Coram,[15] as a home to care for London's many unwanted children. Brook House was a private nursing home where Dr. Monro had full responsibility for the patients, and Tom eventually, took over the duties there from his father. In addition there was one 'safe' house or private house with resident carers, which housed the insane under Monro's supervision, where JR. Cozens was eventually sent. Monro was a patron of artists and found time to involve himself in activities around Bushey. The family seems to have made their summer move out of London towards the end of May, from

1807, not returning to the house at Adelphi Terrace until the middle of October, whilst Monro himself came and went frequently in the whiskey, a high gig, in which he used to drive back and forth from London to Bushey.

Extracts from the diaries make interesting reading, and illustrate for us family life in those days. The doctor was very much a family man. His family correspondence was not frequent, but he wrote to his son Tom when he was at Oxford in Latin, and expected Tom to reply in the same vein. Monro's friends were artists, and few medical colleagues are mentioned as having taken any part in his home life, or as having come to dinner, either in London or the country. That he continued to have a great interest in the artistic world is obvious by the descriptions left by his son and by Farington, although his evening meetings of artists seem to be much more sporadic after the death of Cozens in 1797. A study of his family life reveals some of his further interests, and the importance of his artistic friends, with whom he was so frequently in touch, and who were also frequent visitors at Adelphi Terrace.

The first year of interest from the family point of view is 1807, when on January 13th it is recorded that Daniell, Farington, Hearne, Edridge and Alexander dined. These gentlemen were all part of Monro's 'inner circle' and were frequent visitors to the Adelphi Terrace drawing evenings, the last three often visiting Bushey. This meeting would have been in the London house, where the dining room walls were adorned with 90 drawings, according to Farington, 'framed and glazed, by Hearne, Barrett, Smith and Laporte, Turner Wheatley and Girtin. In the drawing room 120 drawings are hung.'[16] It may have been partly a business occasion, as the next day Henry, the second son, was recorded as receiving his ticket of admission to the Academy Schools. The eldest son, author of the diaries seems still to have been a student at Oxford, but often in

London to record visitors. A careful note of the visitors is sometimes the key towards the Doctor's activities. Tom records in March - after a quiet dinner in Papa's room, Mr Henderson, Lord Essex, Mr. Booth and Dr. Reynolds called. Reynolds was a practising doctor, a family friend, and the one who successfully treated young Tom when as a little boy he had been so ill with whooping cough. Between these dinner engagements, the family went frequently to the theatre, which seems to have been an activity especially popular with Tom and Henry. In April, Hoppner called on 4th. He and Monro were firm friends, whilst his son Lascelles was a frequent visitor to the house. Melford and Wyatt called on 9th April, "to see the drawings". Wyatt was at that time with Nash, one of the busiest architects in England. The month of May seems to have been taken up with Henry's visit to Oxford, although it is recorded that Turner came there, and Henry went into the water with him. The Turner Bequest does not show any drawings from an Oxford visit in 1807. By the end of May, Tom records that he packed up Henry's things, whilst Henry returned to London on the stage (coach.) Tom himself returns early in June, and from the few entries in his diary, this seems to be the first mention of Bushey. Tom records that he went to Bushey on 13th June, 1807, in the carriage with 'Mama and Papa', and that Edridge called on 16th, no doubt eager to see his friend's new house. By 17th June Papa was back in London, in order to dine at the Thatched House club.

The Thatched House club in St. James's Street was founded by Sir Joshua Reynolds, with the help of Johnson, Edmund Burke and Goldsmith, in 1763. They met for supper once a week at seven o'clock (Boswell) but after ten years once a fortnight during the meeting of Parliament. By 1810 it had 76 members, of which over half had been authors. It is recorded that Samuel Rogers put down his name for admission, being already a Member of the Royal Society, but was originally black-balled on account of his politics -

Whig - which seems to indicate that Monro was not a Whig. From the letters of Samuel Rogers it is evident that this was once a literary club, which originally met once a week at the house of Sydney Smith. Monro seems to have been one of the original members, along with Samuel Rogers, Sir James Horner, Mr. Scarlett, Col. Sloper, Mrs. Charles Warren, Richard Sharp, Hoppner, and the two hosts, Mackintosh and Sydney Smith. Gradually a large number of doctors became members, and when Tom was a member, the medical world was well represented as he appeared to go to dinners to meet medical friends. In retirement at Bushey, the old doctor travelled to London almost every month, when he would spend the night with Tom and his wife Sarah, in order to attend these dinners. It was obviously an event at which he met many old friends, and something he looked forward to.

During June, London social life kept everyone busy, and Tom's diary records some of the events for 1807. On 18th Edridge, Alexander, Dickens and Reinagle, two other artists, dined with the Monros. Two days later Benjamin Haydon came to take tea, which was generally something visitors enjoyed in the evening, following dinner. Haydon was a friend to Henry, although older than he was. By 25th June Hoppner, Turner, Edridge and Alexander dined, Turner having returned from Oxford. The following day Tom records that he walked with his mother in the fields toward Watford, having gone 'to stay', or in other words, moved out for the summer. Bushey was only fourteen miles from London. The very next day he went with his mother to Cassiobury, whilst 'Papa went to London.' This is the first mention of Cassiobury, Lord Essex's country house, sometimes spelled by Tom as Cashiobury. Mrs. Monro had presumably, in the fashion of her day, gone to leave her card on the arrival of the family back in residence at Bushey.

During July little of interest is recorded except that Lady C. (Calder) was staying as a patient and Tom wrote that he pasted over the crevices in her floor, and that her servants arrived with their own servants, indicating that she was a guest of some importance. In August most of the Monros were at home at Bushey, with Mr. Hearne and Edridge, and so apparently was Lord Essex, since Henry played cricket there. On the 4th Mr. Edridge went to Cassiobury and Papa and Mr. Hearne dined with Lord Essex. On 11th and 12th August Tom recorded that Papa went to Cassiobury to draw. On 23rd Lady Essex and Mr. Anstey called. He was referred to as "the painter" and occupied the middle portion of Gainsborough's Schomberg house in Pall Mall. September seems to bring much of the same visiting back and forth, but for the first time Bishopsgate Street and Brook House were mentioned, which was the Private Nursing Home administered by Monro, and in fact remained in the family until 1940. By the middle of October Mama and Sally had returned to the Adelphi and Tom was back at Oxford. Just before the family left for London that year, in October, they dined with Mr. Capper at The Manor House, and left the day after. That same day the driveway 'sweep' had been planned, which was the intended entrance in the form of a circular driveway, always entered by the left side, as the carriage swept around in a semi-circle to exit the same way.

The house at Bushey was apparently a newly built "cottage ornee" in the fashionable Regency style, and we know from Tom's diary that many renovations and improvements were done to it by the Monro family, including a new stable, bedrooms on the upper floor, and a new porch added onto the front door. In 1806 the family seems to have spent the summer staying in Barnes with Thomas's brother Charles Monro, and his family before they acquired the house at Bushey. The cousins came to visit at Bushey almost every summer thereafter, especially Fred, Julia and George, children of James, as well as John Boscawen, who was the son of Charles and a good friend to Tom, also Sophy who was the same age as Sally. Henry had a short romance with his cousin Julia, whilst her brother Fred was also a close friend and was the one who accompanied Tom, Henry's brother, to Scotland, when Henry had an accident in falling from his horse when travelling there. Fred was a soldier, in the Royal Artillery, who fought under Wellington in the Peninsular War and at Waterloo. The son of Captain James Monro of the East India Company, Monro's older brother, who later moved to Hadlow, Fred wrote long letters to Tom when he was fighting in the Peninsular War, with detailed descriptions of various battles and events there. Eventually he was to marry his cousin Sally, Doctor Thomas's daughter. Several of the children of both families seem to have been close in age. George was in the navy, and was sadly killed at sea, very young, in the early part of the war against the French.

Meanwhile 'Papa' is written about in Tom's diary as having driven back and forth to London almost daily in the 'whiskey' in those early days at Bushey. By October 4th, 1807, the entry in Tom's diary reports "Dined at home with Mr. Hearne, Edridge and Laporte, indicating the summer visit was over Tom and Henry were great walkers, and on 30th June that year, Tom records that they walked from Bushey to London before breakfast, a distance of fourteen miles. Although they did this journey many times on foot, over the years, notably it is not recorded that it was ever again before breakfast, which was usually held at about ten o'clock in the morning at Bushey.

Young Tom in his life of himself writes that he spent time during the summer at Barnes frequenting 'The Pit'. He writes about various plays, indicating that he and probably Henry, must have often gone there, giving us the clue as to the importance of the theatre to them both. The theatres were important. People attended the opera at His Majesty's Theatre in the Haymarket, where they walked about during the performance visiting their friends. The two great London theatres were Drury Lane and Covent Garden. Here people flocked to see the Kembles, Mrs. Siddons and Edmund Keane, in highly dramatic performances. It was acceptable for young men to jostle together in the pit, as Edward Thomas and Henry Monro must often have done, but once one was 'established' in Society, it was necessary to hire a box. The theatres were not the fashionable rendezvous, since the opera was the more important, and tickets were more readily available for the theatre. There was a marked insularity about London society at this time, cut off as it was by war from the continent, with a great need for the entertainment. Numerous smaller theatres came into being, and successful actors enjoyed high social rank, whilst theatre-going was enjoyed by all levels of society.

In 1808 the summer activities seem to have preceded much as the previous year, with one or two exceptions. The Monro family were doing work to the house, and the Covent Garden theatre burnt down - on 20th September, obviously a major event in Tom's life, as was the destruction of Henry Holland's Drury Lane Theatre the following year. He and his brother Henry seem to have spent every spare moment examining it, both its destruction and re-construction, perhaps forever hopeful of meeting Kemble or some such immortal being. If one can attribute to Monro the background which gave young Turner the discipline of drawing and outline in his art, then it is to his exposure to the theatre, to Gainsborough's late landscapes, the theatrical effects of lighting at the theatre, and finally the exposure to JR. Cozens, all due to his time with Monro, which began to turn Turner's ideas from the more classical influences of Claude and Poussin. An examination of the growing importance of watercolour painting, and an understanding of the importance of the work of JR. Cozens, and the excitement this was to give to Thomas Monro, the family man and busy doctor, must be put in context. The trend from topography to landscape in watercolour can be traced within the space of Monro's life. Many of the artists involved were for a short time students of an evening, at the Adelphi, and as a result formed important friendships. It seems difficult to realise how Monro, a man with an enormous appreciation for drawings, being in touch with so many artists of his day, as well as being an artist himself, had the time and interest to develop the skills of younger men in the medium of watercolour. Girtin also became experienced in drawing in outlines, which perhaps gave him his initial sense of composition, helped by his associations within the Monro circle. The exposure that these young men had to the skills of Henry Edridge, Thomas Hearn and William Alexander, who all gave of their time, was to be of lasting importance, as Girtin drew in outlines, copying engravings or drawings, and Turner coloured in the drawings, according to the fashion of his day. Examples of their work at this stage, show that both were skilled topographical artists in their own right, for example *Durham Cathedral 1796* by Girtin (Whitworth-Univ. of Manchester) and by Turner (1798 R.A.), both from Framwellgate Bridge. A further example might be the interior of *Ely Cathedral* - 1796 by Turner (Aberdeen Art Gall.) of which he did several versions at different times of the day. The doctor's patronage of young artists was not confined to giving them access to his pictures and portfolios of drawings, and letting them make copies, but assisting them with his advice. Exactly how Monro chose his students is not clear, but he proved again and again in his choice, that he had a sharp eye for talent, and having singled out his protégés gave them generous encouragement. These young men formed lasting friendships as a result of meeting at Monro's house on Adelphi Terrace of an evening. The doctor had an extensive library, which we learn from the fact that Tom often recorded cleaning these books. Perhaps it was also at this time that Turner realised, that the poetry of the day, extolling the beauties of the English countryside, could be translated by the painter. He had exposure to the work of Cozens, who had clearly attempted to turn his visual interpretations of the Alps, into the characteristics already established by English prose. Through his Italian scenes he had captured the Italian light and atmosphere, suddenly turning a watercolour painting into far more than just a washed topographical memory.

From his early years Turner was well aware of the romantic tradition found in poetry, and connected this with his painting as early as 1797. He exhibited a sea view at the R.A. which was immediately connected by the critic of *The Times* to Falconer's poem *The Shpwreck.* Literature became a strong influence on many artists, as it had been for the generation before them. Many artists at this time were concerned with poetry and prose, leading to the feeling that 'there is a deal of truth in the notion that our art was verbally framed before becoming visually real'.[17] By 1797-8 the poet Coleridge had written the three works for which he is best remembered, *The Rime of the Ancient Mariner, Kubla Khan* and *Christabel.* Coleridge and William Wordsworth also collaborated on *Lyrical Ballads,* which was credited with beginning the English Romantic Movement. Patrons, such as Monro, would have been well aware of the influence of literature on landscape painting, and the importance of contemporary poets on painters, and their works may well have been under discussion at the house of a man like the doctor who had many books, and was a friend to contemporary men of literature.

During the year of 1809, Tom and his father went to see the *Panorama of Gibraltar,* and later that May to the Panoramas of Cairo and Dublin. The word 'panorama' was first applied to a giant 360 degree painting of Edinburgh, seen from Carlton Hall, by Robert Barker (1739-1806) This was in 1786. Shortly afterwards he found financial backing and by 1793 the Barkers, father and son, opened a permanent building in Leicester Square, showing a full circle view of the Grand Fleet at Spithead. The craze for panoramic views began, not only of *Niagara Falls,* but battlefields and naval engagements. Visitors arriving to view Lord Nelson's attack on Copenhagen, could buy engraved plans to help identify the ships and the whole "phenomenon." The building had an upper deck or circle, so one could walk around to view the scene. Henry Aston Barker, the son of Robert, was at the Royal Academy Schools, knew Turner, also Ker Porter and Henry Monro. Through them he no doubt met Girtin, and they became firm friends. It was Henry Barker who virtually designed all of the earlier panoramic views, whilst Ker Porter was doing scene painting at the Lyceum Theatre, helping with the *Battle of Seringapatam.* Farington notes that on May 3rd, 1799 he went to the Panorama with Barker's view of Windsor painted by the Reinagles. That same year the *Battle of the Nile* was staged. Thomas Girtin was involved in painting some of this scenery, also in painting pantomime scenes for the Covent Garden Theatre, before it burned down. In 1802 Ker Porter produced scenery for the *Battle of Copenhagen,* which Tom Monro records as having gone to see with his brother Henry, and at a later date he took his father. Girtin was also at work on a huge panorama of London, which he began in 1799, executed in tempra, which seems to have achieved a high degree of illusion. Girtin then went to Paris, where in 1801-2 he had been at work on a drop scene used by Tom Dibden, and we can gain some idea of his work since he left several surviving watercolours, drawings and a series of acqua tints. Girtin exhibited his *Eidometropolis* in 1802, months before he died so tragically. For several years he had painted outdoors in all weathers, and it was said that the dampness had eventually weakened his constitution. He was treated by Dr. Monro during his final illness, and the day before he died, begged the doctor :"Only put me in such a way as I can see to continue painting." These descriptions only give an impression as to how important the theatre was not only to the Monro family, but also to the young artists who found employment in painting scenery. Turner seems to have been involved briefly as well, and was probably the artist responsible for the panorama for the *Battle of the Nile,* advertised in *The True Briton,* on 13 June, 1799.[18] Joshua Cristall worked on a view of Constantinople, and he was a friend to Girtin and a pupil of Monro's.

There is no doubt that the theatre, with its new lighting and moving scenery, achieved by rolling up the background on a huge roller, to create a more realistic scene, had an enormous effect on many of these young artists at this time. Transparent stage drops were also used in panoramas. The ideas that were influencing the artists gradually became important to the patron, as they sought out virtuoso displays of painterly effect, as the taste for brightly coloured paintings became fashionable, along with the taste for the picturesque landscape, where the weather suddenly became an important part of the scene. Painters strove to outdo each other in painting stormy clouds, with bright visible rays of sunshine. As new galleries opened up, the competition to create eye-catching, painterly effects was very real, to attract the eye of the art buying public. In addition, the discovery of new paints, especially 'Chinese white', which could be mixed with watercolour paint to create an opaque effect, added considerably to what the painter was able to achieve in this medium.

1. Letters from Mrs. Athelstan Coode (Julia his granddaughter) - private collec.of Dr. F.J.G. Jefferiss - a direct descendant
2. Garlic, Kenneth, editor *Diaries of Joseph Farington* Vol. V 1801-03 Yale Univ.Press 1979
3. letters from Dr F.J.G. Jefferiss - private collection
4. Garlic *Diaries of Joseph Farington* Vol 11 Feb. 1796 p489
5. 'Ibid p489 Farington and Monro dined with Sir George Beaumont, Feb. 1796
6. Garlic *Diaries of Joseph Farington* Vol. IV p2073 July 1803
7. Hertfordshire Local History Council *Hertfordshire Past & Present* No.4 1964 p24
8. Hearne, Thomas w/c Victoria & Albert *Sherwood's Farm, Bushey* also Edridge, Henry *Singer's Farm, nr. Bushey 1811* British Museum w/c. Both works illustrate this period.
9. Foxley Norris D.D. *An Exhibition of Bushey Artists* A Short History of Bushey Artists - article written for an exhibition of Bushey Artists 1769-1969. Ed. Geoffrey Harford.
10. Foxley-Norris, D.D. *Dr. Monro* ibid Exhibition was originally held in Church House, Bushey.
11. Lindsay, Jack *Gainsborough; His Life and His Art* Granada Publishing Ltd. London, New York Sydney 1982 p 104
12. Garlik, K. Ed. The *Diary of Joseph Farington,* Vol. VI - July 5, 1803
13. Pyne. W.H. *Observations on the Rise and Progress of Painting in Water Colours - Repository of Arts,* April 1813 p 219
14. Diaries of Edward Thomas Monro - presented to The British Museum in August, 1960, by P.D.O Coryton, once belonging to Mrs. Coode. These were copied by my aunt, Elmira Wade, by permission of the Keeper of Prints & Drawings at that time, Edward Croft Murray, and these copies are now in my possession.
15. Portrait by Richard Hogarth now at the *Thomas Foram Foundation for Children,* London
16. Ibid Chap. 11 See also Joseph Farington 1796 p 489
17. Sloan, Kim *The Poetry of Landscape - Alexander & John Robert Cozens* Yale Univ. Press. 1986 p162
18. Lindsay, Jack *Turner* Granada Books 1973 p89. Lindsay gives details of other subjects for Panoramas. He also indicates that 1799 was the year Turner's mother came under Monro's care.

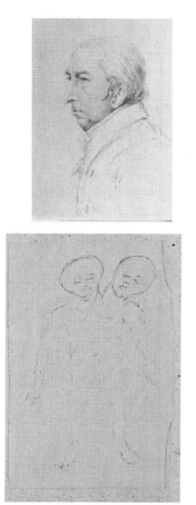

1 A drawing of Thomas
Monro by John
Henderson

Amongst the
Henderson papers – by
kind permission of the
Trustees of the British
Museum

2 A sketch of co-joined
infants from John
Monro to his son Jack.
(family archives

2a A letter from John
    Monro to his son Jack
    – family archives

3. Note from John Monro (son) to his brother Thomas
   (family archives

4. The Adelphi, built by the Adam brothers, 1768-1772.
Note the wharf, and the open vaults under a terrace above.
From an engraving by B. Pastorini from *The Works of
Architecture* by R. and J. Adam

5. St. Mary's Church, Hadley, 1793, by J.M.W. Turner
The house in the background was owned by Dr. Thomas's brother James

6. Scene with Barn, by Thomas Monro (family collection)
Black ink on paper

7. Valley View with Houses by Thomas Monro (family collection)
Black ink and wash on paper

8. Trees on a Hill in a circular frame by Thomas Monro
Black ink/charcoal on paper (family collection

9. View of London from Greenwich by John Varley (private
collection) coloured watercolour

10. Captain James Monro of Hadley by J. Downman, 1789
coloured chalk on paper in the collection of a family descendent.

11. Engraving of Dr. James Monro 1680-1752

12. Engraving of Dr. John Monro – father of Thomas

13. Engraving of Dr. Edward Thomas Monro – elder son.
Born 1789 and known as Tom

14. Engraving of Dr. Henry Monro second son of Edward Thomas
These four engravings are from a single picture showing five
generations of doctors in the Monro family, including Thomas

15. Dr. Monro
visiting his stables at
Bushey after the fire
by William Henry
Hunt. Reproduced
by kind permission
of The Syndics of
the Fitzwilliam
Museum, Cambridge

16. Landscape with a River by Thomas Monro, with kind
permission of the Ashmolean Museum, Oxford.
Black ink and wash

17. Landscape with a Road by Thomas Monro, with kind permission of
the Ashmolean Museum, Oxford.
Black ink and wash

18. Landscape with a Church Tower by Thomas Monro, `with kind permission of the Ashmolean Museum, Oxford.
Black ink and wash

19. A view in the Wood by Thomas Monro, with kind permission of the Ashmolean Museum, Oxford.
Black ink and wash

20. A coloured drawing by Thomas Monro of A Country Inn near a
Pond, with kind permission of the Ashmolean Museum

21. Clandon Park, Surrey – 23rd June, 1827,
by Alexander Monro
Qatercolour – private collection

CHAPTER 4 – THE MONRO CIRCLE

It has been said that there can be no better way to judge a man than through his choice of friends. In the case of Monro, his friends were numerous, but several were especially close, and dined every few days with him at his house on Adelphi Terrace, or he with them. Others were frequent visitors, and the diary of his son, which began in 1806, records many of these visitors. In addition, Monro's students were chosen with care, and he became their friend in most cases, as well as a teacher and adviser, and for this reason the Monro Circle covers more than one generation. Friendships were formed amongst the young artists as well, which were to prove a strong influence on some of their work.

A certain style of work, with watercolour washed over a drawing, often in a grey wash, sometimes blue, has come to be seen as being by the Monro School or Circle. In the search for atmospheric effects with "wiping out" or highlighting in a distinct manner, there were many experiments made in the drawings copied by the students at Adelphi Terrace. In order to realise what influences lay behind many of these drawings, it is important to widen the so called "Circle" and include in it many of Monro's friends, whose influence was not only of great importance to the doctor himself, but also of direct impact on the students. Of these friends perhaps the most important two were Thomas Hearne and Henry Edridge, who were present at many of the evenings when the students met, and allowed their outlines to be copied. It would seem that the printing press at Adelphi Terrace was used to reproduce many of these outlines, so that the students could have practice in colouring them in.

Edward Dayes, also a friend to Monro, to whom Girtin had once been apprenticed, describes the techniques in his writings on *Drawing and Colouring Landscapes in Transparent Colours* in 1805.[1] Here he illustrates the importance put on drawings for the young artist:

"The first thing the young artist must do is to procure some of the best pictures, or drawings, for the purpose of copying: or in lieu of them, some of the best prints: though the latter will not by any means be so useful as the former - every object should be first sketched lightly, and the lines afterwards marked in more vigorously and firmly. No one part of the landscape should be completed before the other." He advises at length about colouring: "and always work from a cold state to a warm one as grey or soft purple may be easily overcome, but a yellow brown, or red, never: then when gone over a second or third time, give the true tone: and lastly, put in the spirited touches, or those touches of shadow in shade, that give animation to the picture."[2] Dayes himself frequently used the picturesque ruin, preferring muted shades of blue and green to wash in his effects.

In his earliest reference to Monro and his Circle, Farington, on 30th December, 1794, mentions in his diary that the outlines of drawings by Thomas Hearne and John Henderson were traced. By far the greater proportion of known Monro School copies are based on outline sketches by JR. Cozens. It has now been proved that Henderson and possibly Dayes, also Hearne and Edridge's work was also used. John Laporte, Monro's teacher was often at Adelphi Terrace, and he may have contributed, since there is a story yet to be proved that he travelled with Girtin on his trip north around this time, to help him with his drawings, since Girtin's drawing of *Plompton Rocks (V&A)*, a pastoral scene with cattle, may given rise to the family tradition that Girtin and he co-operated.[3]   P.J. de Loutherbourg, whose scenery with its theatrical effects was no doubt an influence on both Turner and Girtin, was a friend of the family, and with his very wide continental background gave to his landscapes great theatrical excitement. His work was probably admired by the Monro family, many of whom were frequent visitors to the Drury Lane Theatre, where his highly dramatic transparent backdrops were known to have influenced contemporary painters of landscape. Monro had collected some of Loutherbourg's drawings. Several of Monro's friends might be described as professional picturesque tourists, who looked for specific features in their landscapes, as advocated by the work of Gilpin and Sandby, who educated late eighteenth-century taste, so it is not surprising that Turner's first important tour was made in 1794, the year of his official association with Monro. The doctor it might be said, with the help of his friends, opened Turner's eyes to contemporary taste. In his introduction to his notes on the drawings by Turner, John Ruskin says: "His (Turner) true master was Dr. Monro; to the practical teaching of that first patron, and the wise simplicity of the method of watercolour study in which he was disciplined by him and companioned by Girtin, the healthy and constant development of the youth's power is primarily to be attributed."[4]   In the immediate years following his association with Monro's friends, Turner was to develop a style of drawing in broken outlines and a rather sombre key of colouring, entirely in the spirit of the Picturesque aesthete, with whom he was now in contact. Hearne's work was certainly of influence to Turner when Turner was employed by Monro as a copyist. Meanwhile Girtin, trained by Dayes in the tradition of architectural topography, began to show his ability to capture mood and atmosphere, which greatly added to the architecture of a building. There was little sign of friendship between Girtin and Dayes after Girtin broke his apprenticeship.

Edward Dayes was to write on Turner: "The man must be loved for his works for his person is not striking nor his conversation brilliant. He was born in Maiden Lane, Covent Garden, where his father conducted a decent trade.

Though his pictures possess great breadth of light & shade, accompanied with a fine tone of colour, his handling is sometimes unfirm and the objects are too indefinite: he appears indeed to have but a superficial notion of form.'[5] In spite of these comments Turner won the prize for landscape drawing at the Society of Arts in March 1793 - so it would indicate that in spite of Monro and his friends, Turner early formed a less topographical approach by choice, using pencil drawing only in his sketchbooks. Once he had produced his first oil at the R.A. in 1796, he began to build up his colours with finely graded washes one on top of the other, 'nibbling' through some as he went along to produce different lights. Farington's comment: "Turner has no settled process but drives the colours about until he has expressed the idea in his mind." indicates this.

Thomas Hearne, one of Monro's closest friends, was a pupil of William Woollett. He was an engraver, and apparently had a refined manner of engraving after the style of Richard Wilson. From Redgrave's Dictionary we read that Hearne 'greatly advanced the new art of water-colours. Although weak in colour, his truth and correctness of drawing, his tasteful finish and composition added a new charm to the art. He used the pen sometimes so tenderly in tint that while adding greatly to the minute beauty of his architectural forms, it gives a most delicate sharpness and completion.'[6] Thomas Hearne was born in 1744 near Malmesbury in Wiltshire, and in 1771 Hearne went to the Leeward Islands with Sir Ralph Payne (later Lord Lavington) as draughtsman, and worked on a book of engraved plates with William Byrne entitled *A Contemporary Aspect of Relics of the Past.* Another fifty two subjects by Hearne in *Antiquities of Great Britain* were engraved by W. Byrne and originally cost £1 each. If the origins of British watercolour painting are to be attributed to M.A. Rooker and Thomas Hearne, as art-historians frequently quote, then Paul Sandby must be regarded as

father of the topographical tradition.   Michael Angelo
Rooker, a pupil of Paul Sandby, became a scene designer
for the Haymarket Theatre, whilst Hearne was certainly a
very experienced topographical artist, tending to use ash
greens and shades of grey to wash in his drawings. Hearne
worked for Richard Payne Knight, traveller and writer on
the 'picturesque' view, for a short period, and his work
then took on the essential elements of the picturesque, with
tall framing trees and artfully placed tree stumps, perhaps
to support a rustic bridge, with river and rocks and a
winding path included. Thomas Hearne, we read, 'distilled
the pure prose of the eighteenth-century scene into drawings
for the engravers and his work was admired in the 1790's by
Dr. Monro even above that of the young Girtin and Turner.
By no stretch of the imagination can he be regarded as
having added any marked personal note to the formula
which had been naturalized by Sandby.'[7]   Sandby took a
leading part in the establishment of the Royal Academy, was
an important leader in introducing the topographical
watercolour as a recognised medium, as well as painting
landscapes in watercolour, often showing the influence of
Claude Lorraine Hearne, essentially a man of contemporary
ideas, may not have improved on the style of Sandby, but he
was certainly an artist of consummate skill, and his
influence on the students he came in contact with, including
Sir George Beaumont, was considerable. Hearne was fond
of the picturesque ruins of castles and old abbeys, and
perhaps inspired Turner with this interest. We read often in
the diaries of young Edward Thomas about Hearne, who
was frequently in and out of the house at Adelphi Terrace,
dined there at least once a week during the winter season
and frequently visited the family at their country house,
Merry Hill, in Bushey. Fifteen years older than Monro, he
seems to have been a solemn bachelor, very set in his ways.
Although abstemious himself, Monro remarked to Farington
that he preferred Hearne to drink 3 or 4 glasses of wine, and

there is a legend in the Monro family that after dining at Cassiobury Park, when he was staying at Bushey with the doctor, he was so overcome by the good wine he had consumed, that he was left for the night to sleep it off in the coach house at Merry Hill. Of importance was the fact that he was also often in attendance at the meetings in the evening with the young students. Hearne's influence, because of his accuracy in drawing, certainly affected Turner, and Hearne's method of drawing trees can be seen in early works by Turner. Without doubt his advice must have had an impact on the young students gathered at Monro's house. Monro spent the large sum of £800 upon his collections of Hearne's work. The Doctor told Farington in 1795 that he considered Hearne superior to everybody in drawing.

Another important link with Hearne was Sir George Beaumont, an important collector and *amateur* like Monro, whose own paintings were admired by Farington, and accepted at the Royal Academy. In his diary he writes of Beaumont's landscapes in the Exhibition of 1796: "we have much satisfaction in recording the progressive excellence of this Amateur pencil: its honorary productions this year are 2 landscapes; pure nature charmingly designed and wrought up with all the magic glow of the Flemish school."[8] As a friend and patron of Cozens, and later to Constable, Wordsworth and Coleridge, Beaumont was a central figure in the artistic and literary worlds of the late eighteenth-century and early nineteenth-century in England. Girtin, whose drawings Beaumont collected, and later Constable, were to acknowledge the importance of having been allowed to study Beaumont's collections. The friendship of Monro and Sir George Beaumont caused Beaumont to assign Cozens to Monro's care during his last fatal illness. He wrote several letters to Monro on the subject of Hearne and his illness.

"Mr. Monro   Adelphi Terrace Dunmow   9 Feb. 1815

My Dear Sir:

I have heard an account of our old and valuable friend Hearne which much alarms me. As I take it for granted you attend him you will very much oblige me by giving me some account of him. I have known him well above forty years - and you know him well enough to be aware how anxious all his friends must necessarily be for his welfare.

Our best compls to Mrs. Monro Believe me to be

Most faithfully yours   G.H Beaumont[9]"

Another letter should be quoted in full, since it no doubt indicates some of the feelings that Monro himself must have been under, as Hearne declined in health. Beaumont writes from his Leicestershire seat, Coleorton Hall at Ashby de la Zouche, on December 30, 1816, to Dr. Monro:

"My dear Sir:

I must return you my very best thanks for your account of our good friend Hearne, from which I conclude that altho there appears no immediate danger, yet you think him in decline - he will indeed be a loss to all who know him as an artist and a man. Last year I received a letter from him in which he observes that a friendship of more than forty years standing must necessarily be drawing near its conclusion - a good momento for us both. I first became acquainted with him in the spring of 1771. I came with my tutor Mr. Davy to London and as my fondness for art made me desirous of seeing the most celebrated profesors in every line he carried me to his friend Mr. Woolletts. We mounted up to his garret - and there sat Hearne most assiduously employed in etching from a picture by Swansfeld now in my possession. We passed about six weeks in London and there were few days in which we did not spend some hours in the company of Woollett & Hearne. We talked necessarily of pictures, and plates, and my love for painting was completely confirmed—Mr. Woollett was prevailed upon to promise a visit to Mr. Davy in the course of the summer & bring Hearne with him, accordingly in August they arrived at his house at Henstead in Suffolk. There we passed six weeks together, I may almost say as far as I was concerned in perfect happiness. We sketched all day, & in the evening we delighted with the original pleasantry and inimitable humour of Mr. Davy. I am sure you must have heard Hearne speak of him; we visited Houghton and saw the collection with delight. The remembrance of this happy year near fails when I think of it, to cross my mind like a gleam of bright sunshine. I was young & ardent & admiration, the most pleasing of sensations, I enjoyed in the highest degree. I thought Woollett & Hearne the greatest artists that ever existed - if any one has presumed to say Claude Lorraine or Gaspar knew half so much of the matter, I should have considered it as ignorance or prejudice. Woollett I knew, and regarded to the day of his death, he was an excellant man - it is unnecessary to praise him in his time - since that time, Hearne has daily risen in my esteem - a man of purer integrity does not exist. As an artist where shall we find a more faithful disciple of nature? His sketches are admirable for truth and spirit, & I think I have one of Ely Minster which excells all I ever saw in that line - you remember the drawing he made for me of Tintern Abbey what an excellent performance - By the way I rather think it is at present in his possession - and if you have an opportunity I should be much obliged to yu (to) ask him - I beg your pardon for troubling you at such length, but my subject has run away with me. Poor Hearne! Should we lose him & Alexander in one year - but we must submit - If you should have five minutes to spare, you will gratify me greatly by a line to inform me how he goes on, & what is your opinion of his case - Lady Beaumont unites with me in best compts - to yourself Mrs. Monro & family

I am, My Dear Sir,

Most faithfully yoursG.H. Beaumont[10]

The passionate love for pictures and paintings that possessed Beaumont to the end of his days appears to have been fostered by William Woollett and his apprentice Thomas Hearne. Older than Monro by some six years, it was no doubt the mutual friendship of Hearne, shared with many artistic interests, that brought Beaumont and Monro together. There are certainly several occasions mentioned in Farington's diary when they all met. Beaumont was to write again and ask Monro to provide a nurse to assist Hearne's manservant, for which he would pay. Monro eventually brought Hearne to his house in Bushey to feed him and take care of him during his last illness. When the end came Beaumont could not witness his final departure. The funeral was at Bushey Church, and a tombstone was erected in the churchyard by Monro in memory of his dear friend, whom he buried near his son Henry. The epitaph read:

'Here lieth the remains of Thos. Hearne author of the Antiquities of Great Britain who died the 11th April 1817 in the 73rd year of his age. His character as an artist is sufficiently stamped in his many excellent works. His mind was strong, nervous and independent, his memory clear and retentive, his judgement sound, his manner gentle and conciliating. In short, he possessed more estimable qualities than generally fall to the lot of an individual.'

It is recorded that after a long day at the funeral, Beaumont entertained Dr. Monro, Richard Duppa, Farrington and Hakewill to dinner at Grosvenor Square. Hearne appointed

Henry Edridge and Monro his Executors, and left in his will '£50 to Thomas Monro M.D. and the cabinet in my bedroom, and to the aforesaid Dr. Thomas Monro £800 in Trust - 3% consolidated annuities and any interest there from for the sole use of William Baker, son of Ann Baker my late faithful domestic' It is evident from this that Hearne trusted the Doctor rather than a fellow artist to carry out his wishes. It was always supposed that William Baker was Hearne's natural son.

Henry Edridge also shared a close bond of friendship with Monro, and was in constant touch with him, and like Hearne visited Adelphi Terrace frequently, and was often a part of the meetings that took place with the students in the evening there. He was born in 1768, and became a pupil of William Pether, engraver in mezzotint, and spent much of his apprenticeship in drawing portraits, becoming a student at the Royal Academy Schools in 1784, where he won a silver medal for drawing from the antique.   In 1786, Joshua Reynolds allowed him to make copies of his own works in miniature, an art at which he excelled in his early days, first working with black lead or India ink. Redgrave's Dictionary describes his art as having a great feeling for landscape art which he derived from a study of Hearne, whom he surpassed in colour. Edridge was musical, often sang whilst Sally Monro accompanied him on the piano, and added a great deal to the evenings at the Monros, being very outgoing. He and Monro exchanged frequent letters. Edridge often painted with Hearne at Bushey, during the early 1800's, either as a guest of the Monro family, both at Fetcham and at Bushey, or of Lord Essex at Cassiobury. He also made portraits of Monro, and as a miniaturist, several of Monro's family. He went to Paris in 1817, commenting on the fact that Monro had just returned from there in one of his letters. He wrote to Monro in September 1817, that he had had a most pressing invitation from Sir Abraham Hume "to accompany him in an excursion to Paris and thro'

Flanders. I at first declined it, but he has repeated the attack and I can hardly resist the temptation, the circumstance of going so easily and comfortably with scarce any charge and with an agreeable and friendly companion is perhaps more than I ought to refuse." He went again in 1819 to accompany Sir George Beaumont, whom he found 'a perpetual fidget: tiresome to the greatest degree - all doctrine and no practise'[11] They were however evidently good friends., and Edridge writes again in September, 1819, to say that he presumes Beaumont has returned from his travels 'as I had notice from him today in the shape of a brace of birds.' Hearne, Edridge and Alexander were in the habit of dining together at the Monro's at least once a month, as is recorded in Edward Thomas's diary, and there are entries that Edridge sang from time to time. Letters from this period until 1820 report on the two trips Edridge made to France, and then in 1816 on the sad loss of their mutual friend Alexander, who died in the care of his brother in Maidstone, Kent, a few months before Hearne.

Dr.Monro   Bushey

Wed. 24th July, 1816

My Dear Friend:

I am shocked beyond measure to tell you that poor Alexander is no more. There is a letter come from his brother stating his end to have taken place yesterday morning. How truly awful. How useless now to regret he went to Maidstone where perhaps he was not properly treated, but I scarcely know what to think or say - he was an excellent fellow - may his change be blessed.

I hope to see you Saturday. I am required to attend his funeral. I am most deeply distres'd

Yours

Edridge writes again, presumably a week later:

Dr Monro   Bushey Tuesday   Margaret Street

My Dear Friend:

I was in some hope's I shld have seen you today here -1
have promised to go on Friday next to Bromley to stay
till Monday, after that I shall be glad when convenient,
to you to come & see you. I have just seen Lord Essex
here and have agreed to go to him as soon as I have
been with you -1 could not go to the Adelphi last night
as I had someone here. My spirits are in a sad state
                    Ever yours most truly   H.
                    Edridge

Another letter addressed to Doctor Monro, written from
Hanwell on Monday morning, April 14, 1817, despairs
over the death of his friend Hearne:

Dear Friend:

The moment I saw the face of Mr. Burton I knew all
was oer. I fear's it would be so and that I shld. never
more see my excellent old friend alive - deeply as I
regret it, perhaps under the circustances in wh. I feel
myself it is best that I did not witness with you his final
departure. It is some consolation that you did - you
have proved his constant friend to the last moment.
Thus is our little social band melting fast away as all
human affairs must -Alas! poor Hearne.

I was preparing to go to Town I am not sure now
whether I can get there today - if not I shall see you
tomorrow. We will then take the necessary steps this

melancholy event requires - I am ill calculated for such offices at present. If the day turns out favorable I may see you today - God bless you my Dear friend. The time we have allow'd us we must pass as much together as we can.

Faithfully yours,   H. Edridge

In less than a year Edridge had lost two great friends, as had Monro.

On September 14th, 1817, Edridge's letter begins with a reference to Dr. Monro's return from France. He appears to have made only a short stay 'to settle his boys in Boulogne'. This no doubt referred to Alexander and John, since Tom married in 1814, the year Henry died, and Bob was also married. Edridge refers to a pressing invitation he has had to accompany friends to Paris, and appears to be in a state of indecision, although eventually he did go.

"I wish very much to have some talk with you - first of all I shd. like much to know how you have left your Boys established and am strongly tempted to trust mine upon the same plan tho' I see many difficulties to overcome." Edridge ends the letter "Pray have you a travelling cap you once lent me." He wrote from France Mon cher Frere, in a letter telling of his adventures in Rouen and Paris. "I often think of you and wish you could see with me the extraordinary things that France produces. Magnificence and filth - the formal and the picturesque there abound."

These extracts help us to understand the close bond that existed between the two friends. During the following year he travelled with his son Henry to Taunton, from where he wrote to Monro:

"The journey so strongly advised was perhaps the worst thing I could have done - it is too late to repent. It is impossible I can leave him while he is in this state." He wrote again to Monro on July 1, 1818, still in Taunton: "I have the most dreadful prospect before me and must learn to bear it. I cannot find resolution to state what is useless to distress you with. I have desired Hakewell to call upon you when he gets to London. He will tell you what I cannot. (His son Henry had died from consumption.) I am sorry to learn your son John still continues to give you uneasiness & I am sorry to be cut off from the society of friends that I love, who I must look for in the future for consolation under circumstances of the most afflicting nature. I know all that can be said upon the subject of submission, but I feel it will be as much as I shall be able to support." By 25th July he wrote: "All is finished indeed. The dear sufferer is released from the extremity of human misery. He expired at $\frac{1}{4}$ past one this morn." Edridge finishes the letter "let me have the comfort of hearing from you soon."

The sadness seems to have affected Edridge's own health, and further letters from this year complain of his cough and digestion. Another trip to Paris the following year with Sir George Beaumont, finished with him travelling to Normandy to sketch. He had managed to send 'a slip of paper' to Alexander Monro in Boulogne, which was an act of kindness for a friend. The two trips to France however did not cure his health, nor improve his sadness. By Saturday, April 21 of 1821 the following letter was sent by Monro's son, Edward Thomas, who was by then a practising doctor.

Dr. Monro   Bushey   Watford   Herts.

My dear Father:

95

I have just heard from Mr. Hakewill that poor Edridge is so much worse today that Baillie and Kenison do not expect him to survive till the morning -I fear his legs have mortified.

Most affly yr   E.T Monro[12]

33 Bedford Place Russell Square

This letter indicates that the King's Physician, Dr. Baillie, had been brought in to care for Edridge by Monro. Farington wrote that "he complained of pain from the left shoulder to his wrist", which Dr. Monro said was one of the symptoms of 'Aneurism, a disorder about the heart'. Further reports followed on a daily basis. Henry Edridge died on 23 April, 1821, Monro buried him at Bushey Church and had a tombstone constructed for him there. The inscription on his tomb read:

'To the memory of Henry Edridge A.R.A. An artist of distinguished talent and a man of a benevolent and tender heart, polished manners and unsullied integrity. The loss of an only daughter in her seventeenth year and afterwards of an only son of the same age pressed upon his spirit and he died on the 23rd April, 1821 aged 52 years.'

When he writes to his father it is interesting that Tom refers to him as "our poor friend", and indeed he had been such a long time friend to all the family, seen the children growing up, and such a regular visitor to dinner or of an evening that it would be quite natural for the children to regard him as their friend also. The letters tell of the affection Edridge had for Monro, and in others he mentions again his frequent need to see his old friend. Edridge at least died knowing that he had been elected as an associate of the Royal Academy, to his great pride.

William Alexander was a very good friend to Monro, often present at the gatherings at Adelphi Terrace, although not so frequently at the evening meetings when students were using the house. He was born in 1767 in Kent, the son of a coachmaker. He trained with William Pars, and in 1784 became a student at the R A schools, where presumably he became acquainted with the young Edridge. In 1792 he sailed with Lord McCartney's mission to China as a topographer and draftesman. He returned to begin work at the British Museum as assistant Keeper for 'antiquities', and eventually became Keeper of Prints and Drawings. He is described as a man of cultivated tastes, an artist, antiquary and connoisseur. As such he clearly was a man whose company Dr. Monro enjoyed. He went to his brother's house in West Mailing in Kent in 1816, and there suffered from a stroke. There are letters from his local doctor to Monro to ask his advice, which Monro declined to give, not being there to examine the patient, but advised that blistering of the head, bleeding and purging were the correct treatments. Alexander died shortly after this.

In the early diaries of Edward Thomas, from 1806 and 1807, two other visitors are recorded quite frequently as having called. One was Mr. Laporte and the other Mr. Reinagle. In December of 1795 Monro is recorded as having mentioned to Farington that he 'proposed to sell part of his collection of drawings, as he thinks he has too many Laportes etc' He seems to have not taken any action on this comment since we learn in 1803 from Farington that Monro told him that he had purchased drawings from Laporte to the value of £500 to £600. He also mentions that Laporte made soft ground etchings of Gainsborough's drawings of which Monro had a large number. There is certainly plenty of evidence that Monro himself drew in a similar style, and since he began to take lessons from Laporte the year that he married, in 1789, and continued these for several years, it is not surprising that they drew on the same source of inspiration. He was a friend, came often to dinner, visited Bushey in October, 1809, and possibly on other occasions.

There is an entry in Tom's diary for that same year, for December 24 that Mr. Henderson dined and admired Laporte's Gainsboroughs. John Laporte died in 1839, and although there is less mention of him in the diaries as the years pass, this is because Tom himself was taken up by his own life and was not such a frequent visitor himself to Adelphi Terrace. Laporte first appeared as an exhibitor in 1785 at the Royal Academy, and was apparently a constant contributor of landscape scenery. Another friend, Philip Reinagle, was born in 1749, attended the schools of the Royal Academy in 1769 and was employed by Ramsay, the portrait painter, where he assisted in numerous repetitions of royal portraits. Redgrave's Dictionary notes that initially, until 1785, the work he exhibited at the Royal Academy was exclusively portraits. From that time he tried animal paintings with great success, and from 1794 he painted chiefly landscapes and seascapes. Perhaps this was the year that he met Monro, and began to appreciate some of the ideas of those who gathered at his Adelphi Terrace house. He died the same year as Monro, aged eighty-four. Reinagle certainly was caught up in the excitement of the theatre of the time, and possibly in the great demand for theatre scenes, as was his son Ramsay. (1775-1862). Ramsay attended the R A schools with Henry, as well as Monro's Friday evening gatherings, but no evidence appears as to which years. Farington notes in his diary in 1799 that he went to see the Panorama of Windsor, with the view painted by the Reinagles.[13] This does not make it clear as to what part they exactly played, was it as scenery painters or in painting a view of Windsor, as a part of the whole production. What is recorded is that in the early 1800's Reinagle senior was a visitor on several occasions to the house lived in by the Monro family Henry Monro is recorded as having gone to see Miss Reinagle on 19th August, 1809 It would seem that Monro's children knew both the son and daughter of Philip Reinagle. Ramsay, his son, exhibited with the Water-Colour Society in 1806 and 1807, and was elected a member of the Society.

John Henderson was also certainly a part of the circle of friends who came and went in those early years, and appears to have settled into the Adelphi at about the same time as the Monro family, living at No. 3 or 4. He also had a young family, and Monro celebrated with him in 1797 at the birth of his son. Henderson was also a lover of drawings and had a large collection, including at least four by Canaletto, which Girtin and Turner were allowed to copy. Roget mentions that Turner copied from Hearne, but Girtin preferred the Canaletto and Piranesi.[14]   A view of London by Canaletto, owned by Henderson, was copied many times by Girtin, and it is said that in this manner he began to appreciate the shorthand used by this artist, and also to understand his picturesque qualities. Farrington wrote in his diary, in 1795, "after tea I looked over a Portfolio of outlines of Shipping and boats made at Dover by Henderson. Very ingenious and careful.   We staid till past Eleven o'clock. Turner and Girtin were not in Dover themselves, but copied drawings made by Henderson."[15 & 16]   In his earliest reference to the Monro circle, Farington says that the outlines - here those of Thomas Hearne and John Henderson, were traced; this has been accepted by art historians, but it is not recorded as to how much time Girtin and Turner spent drawing at his house.[17]   Several views from Monro's sale on views of Dover were no doubt made by Girtin at this time, and kept by Monro. It seems very unlikely that Girtin travelled to the Cinque Ports, (including Dover) on tour with James Moore in 1795 as has been suggested.[18]   Henderson was certainly a very important amateur artist and patron, and a friend, like Monro, to many of the artistic names of his day. Perhaps he was helpful in introducing Girtin to some members of Society, since Girtin's patrons by the end of his career encompassed the cream of Georgian society.[19]   Through

Thomas Monro, Sir George Beaumont, Lord Essex and John Henderson, all of whom were enthusiastic supporters, Girtin was passed on to Edward Lascelles, son of one of the richest men in England, where he was eventually given his own studio at Harewood. Both Lascelles and Lady Gower, Countess of Sutherland, took lessons from Girtin. She later recalled; 'he used to point out the time of the day, the cast shadows and particular effect suited to the time and scene etc. a mode of teaching far in advance of the time.'[20] Such ideas were exactly what the skills of the artists associated with Monro were able to impart. It was John Henderson's son who gave his father's collection of drawings, including several by Girtin and Turner, to the British Museum. In the early years many of the outlines traced by the young artists were possibly done by Henderson, since Girtin's grandson wrote: "By far the greater proportion of known Monro School Copies are based on outline sketches by J.R. Cozens, Henderson and probably Dayes."[21] A letter exists, written by Henderson on the illness of his daughter, to Monro, which begins "My dear Friend". He writes about her rheumatic gout, which was "translated" to the heart, and she died. This is dated December 8, 1819, and he ends "May you henceforth be strangers to sickness and sorrow, ever and faithfully yours, John Henderson."[22] This does indicate that Monro and Henderson were indeed neighbours who were on friendly terms, sharing family joys and sorrows.

Monro was obviously a man who derived much pleasure from associating with the younger generation and helping them with their drawings and watercolours. John Sell Cotman (1782-1842) arrived in London probably sometime in 1798, aged sixteen, and on December 15th Farrington recorded that 'Dr. Monro is bringing forward another young man who comes from Norwich.' Having moved to London, Cotman supported himself by colouring prints for

Ackermans, the print seller. Sir Harry Englefield who was a patron of Cotman, was also a friend to Monro. In the Monro sale of 1833 one of the lots was a 'Bundle of very early sketches by J.S. Cotman'. His earliest sketches show how powerfully he was influenced by Girtin. He may have worked with Girtin along with a group of young artists who were gathered together by Sir George Beaumont at Conway in 1800. Farington mentions that many of Monro's friends and pupils stayed at Fetcham with him, and drew in the district, including Turner, Varley, Cotman, Hoppner, Edridge and Hearne. Farington was there in July of 1803. Again Redgrave's Dictionary mentions that Cotman frequented the well-known artists' meetings at the house of Dr. Monro. Cotman was certainly a part of the sketching club, founded by Francia and Girtin, which will be seen to have included many friends of Girtin's made from his associations with the Monro group of young artists.. In 1807, having been refused Membership to the Old Water-Colour Society, he returned to Norwich and became a member and the secretary of the Norwich Society of Artists, and began to paint in oils. Cotman was to join the Watercolour Society as an Associate in 1825. Meanwhile he became a friend of Girtin's and of Peter de Wint. Thomas Girtin, the grandson of the artist mentions that on Cotman's death (1842) not one obituary appeared. He was thought of only as a poor drawing master in Norwich. Since then he has been described as one of the World's greatest watercolourists. There is no doubt that his happiest period was from 1805 to 1812 when his greatest brilliance was achieved. He went to Yorkshire in 1803 and again in 1805, where he stayed with the Cholmeley family of Brandisby Hall, who introduced him to local society, whose children he taught to draw. . Turner persuaded Cotman to direct his energies towards the architectural antiquities of Norfolk and Normandy. His awareness of light and shade he learnt from Girtin, as well as the abstract structure of the English countryside.. He employed the dot and dash technique in his drawing common to the circle of young artists associated with Dr. Monro, as did William Henry Hunt, and was close to Henry Edridge in style. The grandson of Girtin wrote: Cotman's style was to reduce landscape to its essentials and to compose the scene from flat shapes of colour fitted together like jigsaw pieces - with stems and branches silhouetted against dark, and the technique of taking out the colour by blotting or scraping to create better lights.[23]

Peter De Wint (1784-1849) already knew Girtin from their days spent copying at Raphael Smith's, colouring in engravings and mezzotints, and he became well known to the elder Monro boys, as he took part in the Friday evening meetings.. Tom's diary records several visits when De Wint came for tea, and he visited Bushey on two occasions in 1807 and 1809, playing cricket and going to church with the family. By this time he was no longer a pupil. However during the early 1800's students seem to continue in the practise of coming of an evening, including Hunt and even John Varley, to colour in drawings. However, it would seem more likely that Varley was later used in an advisory capacity, since he took on De Wint as a pupil. Peter De Wint went to Fetcham at various times to sketch with Dr. Monro, and he found inspiration in the drawings of Girtin, which became a lasting influence and supplied his sense of colour. He is known for his paintings in watercolour of the flat countryside around Lincoln, where he went to live. Fetcham Cottage was near Leatherhead in Surrey. Around 1796 Monro rented a house here, of little architectural merit, according to Joseph Farington, where many of his pupils and friends stayed , going out to draw in the district, including Turner, and the two Varley brothers. John Varley went in 1799 and 1800 to Fetcham, 'to make coloured sketches in the neighbourhood, particularly about Box Hill'.   Roget further informs us: "For the advantage of being near this valued seat of art learning, John Varley, at Dr. Monro's suggestion, came in the year 1800, into that painter's old familiar neighbourhood, and took up his abode with his brother Cornelius in Charles Street, Covent Garden. Here the good doctor visited Varley, was delighted with his progress, in which he took great interest, standing by while he drew and dictating the tints he should use."[24] Varley, who was a founder and a prominent member of the Old Water-Colour Society became one of the most important teachers of his generation. His pupils included David Cox, Linnel, De Wint, and William Mulready. There is a study from nature done by Varley at this time made in company of Dr. Monro, dated October 1800 (Laing Art Gallery - Newcastle) There appears to be little of Varley's style in this, but a great deal of Monro's. However, the drawing does indicate how he took his young friends, including Varley, out into the area around Fetcham, to study directly from the countryside. The trees show the influence of Sandby, but the flat panoramic distance with its striped fields and dotted trees is pure Girtin, and suggests that Monro held up Girtin as the best example for his young protégé to follow. Farington further recorded in his diary, on November 2nd, 1802, "Dined at Dr. Monro's. Much was said about the singularities of Varley, an ingenious young man who has been making drawings in Wales." Cornelius Varley (1781 -1873) joined his elder brother John in frequenting the Adelphi Terrace meetings about 1800. He also visited Fetcham, and almost certainly made his copy of J.R. Cozen's *From the Myrth Plantations of Sir William Hamilton's Villa at Portia* whilst at Adelphi Terrace, where he also copied unfinished water colours by Cozens. His drawings of *West Humble Lane* would have been started while staying at Fetcham, although they are dated 1806, and Dr. Monro gave up the cottage late in 1805. Cornelius worked from Nature, like his brother John, but was never such a prolific artist. He invented a "graphic telescope", which projected the chosen image flat on a table. John Varley made portraits with the help of this device, one of which is inscribed: "Dr. Monro - the first collector of Turner and Girtin's drawings. Done with a graphic telescope, April 12th, 1812." John Constable wrote that John Varley had called on him, and he bought a little drawing from him. Apparently Varley encouraged Constable "to do landscape, and was so kind as to point out my defects. The price of the drawing was a guinea and a half to a gentleman, and a guinea only to an artist", but Varley insisted upon Constable taking the larger sum, although Constable wrote "he had clearly proved to me that I was no artist."[25]   Varley must have been a kindly man, since he even gave lessons at 5 a.m. to a John Dobson of South Shields, rather than disappoint him. Certainly he was very hardworking, and a prolific artist, which is how he is regarded to this day.

Joshua Cristall (1768-1847) was also a pupil at Monro's, although considerably older than most of the students, and became a founder member of the Old Water-Colour Society, as well as a friend to John Varley. He was a shy and quiet man, and his subjects were wide ranging , but Redgrave's Dictionary describes that he entered an apprenticeship with Dr. Monro. He had entered the Academy Schools in 1795, and was helped by the guidance and friendship of Monro. He was President of the Old Water Colour Society in 1816, 1819 and 1821, and during his lifetime contributed well over three hundred works to its exhibitions. John Linnell (1792-1882) was also a part of this group and we read in Tom's diary that in November, 1806, Linnell, Hunt and Turner came to draw.   In Thomas Girtin's description he mentions that Turner's *Liber Studiorum* in imitation of Claude's *Liber Veritas* was not begun until 1807, so perhaps Turner was copying or even collecting some of his former efforts in anticipation of his future work. Linnell in his autobiography of 1863 said that he went to Dr. Monro's with Hunt and that they were paid l/6d per hour. He mentions that he later paid Monro £45 for five drawings by Cozens and Girtin, and also brought away a folio of his old drawings. On 22nd February, 1806, he records that he was at Dr. Monro's and 'saw Gainsboro's Show', when he appears to have attended at Dr. Monro's house about once a week, but sometimes on two consecutive days.. It is interesting to read his journal for February and March of that year indicating that he was on good terms with Tom and Henry, and Monro himself. Monro also arranged for the young Linnell to be apprenticed to John Varley, along with De Wint. Copley Fielding must also have been a member of the group of young artists meeting at Adelphi Terrace about 1800, but we hear little about him, although we know that Ruskin held him in high regard.

William Henry Hunt (1790-1864) would have been the same age more or less of the Monro boys. Roget mentions that' Hunt often stayed with the Doctor at Bushey for a month at a time and was paid by him 7/6d a day for the drawings he produced.'[26]   He was there in the summer of 1815, arriving on 17th August, and during the next few days making sketches and 'watercolour drawings' of the stables and the house.   Tom records that on 6th October, 1807, writing "Young Hunt to draw" at Adelphi Terrace.   In 1816 Hunt arrived on July 20th, and was still there on September 5th, when Tom wrote:" The boys went to St. Albans with Mr. Hunt." Being a cripple, it must have been difficult having to be trundled about in a barrow, even if it did have a hood. He seems to have remained on friendly terms with Tom who records that he went to exhibitions staged by Hunt in London on several dates after this, as Hunt developed his painstaking style of detailed studies in the form of still lives of fruit, flowers and birds' nests. Ruskin recommended Hunt as the best model to his students of watercolour painting. Hunt's ability to describe the literal appearance of his subject appealed to an age fascinated with science, who admired realism and accuracy. He used body colour to highlight detail and achieve a balance of light and shade, and exhibited at the Old Water-Colour Society. There is a description of Monro at Bushey going on a sketching trip with Hunt, and when he became frustrated because Hunt was unable to achieve the right tints, he lifted him out of his buggy onto the ground, and then proceeded to seat himself in the contraption, and show the young man how to achieve the desired result in his drawing.

The artists may have been very young, but important friendships were formed, and these were to be useful in a society where there was much interaction between professional artists. This is clear when a study is also made of the membership of the sketching society formed by Louis Francia and Girtin in 1799, called The Brothers of the Brush. The group consisted of Worthington and Thomas Girtin, J.C. Denham, the Treasurer, Louis Francia, the Secretary, Thomas Underwood, Robert Ker Porter and George Samuel, also Joshua Cristall. Although this group offered each other social support, they were serious in their aims. 'Porter had been a fellow with Turner at the Royal Academy Schools, where he and Henry Aston Barker were 'great companions and confederates in boyish mischief,' to the 'botheration' of Wilton the Keeper.   Barker was the son of an Irish artist who introduced Panoramas to London. Porter himself had been admitted to the schools at the age of 13, and two years later won the silver palette of the Society of Arts for history painting. Worthington and Denham were amateurs, the former a pupil of Girtin. Underwood was an amateur in the group having worked at Dr. Monro's at some point.'[27]   Louis Francia (1772-1839) was born in Calais, and became an assistant at J.C. Barrow's Drawing School. While still an assistant to

Barrow, he was apparently also a fellow student with Girtin at Dr. Monro's and his drawings made at the club meetings are almost indistinguishable from those of Girtin. He worked in the medium and manner of Dr. Monro[28] we are told. The group met on Saturday evenings at 6 o'clock and worked until ten, just as they had done at Monro's, illustrating a selected passage of poetry. It is interesting that Turner was not a member, although J.S. Cotman later joined, as did AW. Callcott, pupil of Hoppner, so that all these friends had met at Dr. Monro's or knew each other from being fellow artists at the R.A schools, so forming a tightly knit social group. It is possible that Turner did not want to join as he would not be able to invite the group to his house, since the group met at each other's houses or lodgings. It was during these years that his mother was growing increasingly violent, making home life very difficult, before she was removed to Dr. Monro's care, or perhaps he was just to taken up with his growing career and imminent move to Harley Street. He was never a joiner, often being described as difficult and rude, so this may have been an added reason. The host of the night did have to supply strained papers, colours, pencils as well as refreshments. It was this group who began to be caught up in the fascination of the panoramic scenes becoming so popular at the theatre, which was to lead to further developments by the turn of the century.

We think of many of these men as becoming classic leaders of the English School of Water-colour, and perhaps as a result of their association the foundation of the first society specifically dedicated to watercolour was set up in 1804. Ten painters in water-colour, Roget described in his History, met together at the Stratford Coffee House on Oxford Street, on 30th November, 1804, and there united themselves into an associated body and drew up a set of rules. At the same time they formally assumed the title of the Society of Painters in Water-Colours. It was to consist of no more than twenty four members, and Gilpin was initially installed in the chair. Both Varley brothers were members. Apparently the experiment succeeded "beyond the most sanguine expectations."[29] The first exhibition opened on 22 April, 1805, at 20 Lower Brook Street, which had been built as a showroom by Gerard Vandergucht. The exhibitions were crowded, and in the seven weeks that it remained open, nearly twelve thousand people paid for admission. John Varley sent 42 works, and Joshua Cristall sent 8. The main strength of the collection lay in its landscapes, so the change that had come over 'water-colour drawing' could clearly be seen.

Monro and his Circle of artistic friends had exposed many artistic young men to a breadth of treatment and an instinct for colour and atmosphere that was entirely new in water-colour paint. They oversaw their drawing, and by allowing them to copy from so many famous artists such as Canaletto and Gainsborough, and in particular J.R. Cozens, certainly inspired them, and then the trained eyes of Hearne and Edridge taught them about tints and colours. Monro himself encouraged them to look to Nature, and to draw directly out in the countryside. Each man brought different talents, and their association with pupils or friends further broadened the circle. Turner and Girtin certainly formed a lasting friendship, tragically broken by Girtin's early death in 1802, aged only twenty-seven when Turner is said to have remarked, 'If Tom Girtin had lived, I should have starved.'

1. Dayes, Edward *The Works of he Late Edward Dayes.* London 1805 pub. Mrs. Dayes, 42 Devonshire St. Queen Square
2. Ibid p282-283
3. Girtin, D & Loshak, D. *The Art of Thomas Girtin* A&C Black, London 1954 p32
4. Ruskin, John *The Lamp of Beauty: Writings on Art* Phaidon Press 1995 pi 86-7
5. Dayes, E. 1805 p352
6. Redgrave, S *A Dictionary of artists of the English School* Bell & Son, London 1878
7. Reynolds, Graham *Watercolours* Thames & Hudson, London 1992 p57-58
8. Garlic, K. ed. *The Diaries of Joseph Farington Vol* 11 p639 (1796)
9. Letters from Mrs. Coode at the British Museum. See also *Collector of Genius* by Felicity Owen, 1998p152p190 see BM file: 1973-12-18-17
10. Letters from Mrs. Coode at the British Museum
11. Ibid - written to Monro from Paris, dated June 17, 1819
12. All quotations taken from the letters of H. Edridge are from material in the Coode file
13. Garlic, Kenneth Ed. p1216May3, 1799
14. Roget, J.L. *History of the Old Water-Colour Society* pp86.87
15. Garlic, K. ed. *Diaries of Joseph Fanngton* p420 Vol.11 11ᵗʰ Dec. 1795
16. Croft-Murray E. Br.M. Quarterly, Vol X 1935 The tracing was done by placing the
17. drawing over glass.
18. Bell C.F Walpole Society XXI11 1934-5 p22
19. Bell. C.F. Walpole Society Vol. 5 1915-16 edited A.J. Finberg p75-76
20. Hill, D. *Thomas Girtin - Genius in the North* Harewood House Trust 1999 p8
21. Ibid p9
22. Girtin, T and D. Loshak *-The Art of Thomas Girtin* 1954 p31
23. Letters from Mrs. Coode at the British Museum
24. Girtin, Thomas *The Antique Dealer & Collectors Guide* Sept. 1982 p.64
25. Roget *History of the Old Water-Colour* Society *Vol.1 pp77-9*
26. Taken from a notebook by Randall Davies
27. Ibid pp392-393
28. Lindsay, Jack *Turner* Granada Books 1981 p87
29. Roget, Vol 1 p99

30. Roget, Vol I,pl 75& p203

CHAPTER 5 – TOM, HENRY & SALLY MONRO

Reflected in the diaries of Tom, a great deal can be learned about the everyday life of an artistic and educated family, not part of Society, yet involved in many contemporary events, and associated with many contemporary artists. Monro himself appears restless and busy, and scarcely a day passed when it is not recorded that Papa came or went, covering his busy practice no doubt, arranging life at Bushey, and finally consulting at Windsor, when called to do so by those caring for King George III. His eldest son Tom was reliable and hardworking, quite the opposite of his artistic brother Henry, although the two were very close, and the doctor came to rely on Tom increasingly as the years passed. Sarah, or Sally, seemed to hold the family together, since her excitable mother was often unable to cope, and we read she would frequently retire to her room when life became too exciting.

Family life involved not only a busy practice, but considerable pressure being put upon Tom as his family began to reach adulthood. The doctor himself was very indulgent towards his family, and seemed to deny them very little. Monro evidently sought repose in many of his sketches: they suggest an escape from the disturbances of his own family and his professional life, and a delight in the play of sunshine and shade on trees, since trees form the major part of his studies. There is no doubt that the house at Bushey was of great importance to the entire family. Little is mentioned by Tom as to why the area was chosen and correspondence between Lord Essex and Monro has not come to light, but undoubtedly it was because of their mutual friendship. The two friends visited back and forth frequently, with Monro's family always welcomed at Cassiobury, as were their guests. The family met the neighbours, The Cappers, the Ansteys, Mr. Haliburton and the Reverend Vivian and his wife, and again all were invited both to dinners at Cassiobury and Merry Hill. The Monro children went to Cassiobury to play cricket in the summer, although Tom, who was not as keen a player as his brother Henry, does not tell us who made up the teams. It would appear that Dr. Thomas had little time to join in these games, but certainly Essex did from time to time. Uncle Charles visited quite frequently, during the summer months, as did his daughter Sophie, a particular friend of Sally Monro. Charles's son John Boscawen, was a great friend to both Harry and Tom, being some three years younger than Tom. His name appears quite often in Tom's diary, and he certainly carried on a frequent correspondence with 'Bos', who later became a Barrister. They remained friends long after they were established in their chosen careers, and there are entries in the diary about Bos coming for dinner. The Hadley Monro cousins, the children of James, especially Frederick, Julia and George, also Charlotte, who eventually married Bob, and was the youngest of the four, visited in the summers. Fred was a particular friend to Henry, and two years younger than Tom. His sister Julia was a friend to Sally, and was a frequent visitor, and had a short romance with her cousin Henry. In September, 1809, Julia, Charlotte and George were staying, and Fred is recorded as having returned 'from the wars and Woolwich.' The young cousins at Bushey all went to the Stanmore Ball. Henry was also painting Julia, and seems to have lost his heart to his young cousin. Meanwhile Fred wrote many letters, especially to Tom, which have been kept by the family, listing events in Spain where he fought in the Battle of Salamanca, and stayed to witness the defeat of the French there. He was a lieutenant in the Royal Artillery and kept a diary of events leading up to the great battle of Waterloo. He was also called upon by the family to go with Tom to rescue Henry from Scotland, when he fell ill, and also to bring Alexander back from his attempted elopement. It was Fred who eventually married his first cousin, Sally Monro, but it was a childless marriage. George joined the navy and was killed in action near Sicily in 1812.

The diary of Edward Thomas has many routine notes concerning the daily lives of the Monros and their friends, and is of interest in that these indicated the social and political concerns of the early part of the nineteenth-century. Tom gives a vivid picture in his notes as to how they lived and what they achieved in a day - also how they travelled. Of course there was domestic help, a new footman, cook who travelled to Bushey every summer, and a coachman, all being mentioned. Madam, which is how he referred to his mother, and Sally are not recorded as doing any household chores, but Monro himself 'papered and carpeted after the workmen had finished', at Bushey, whilst Henry hung the Drawing Room mirror, and more drawings. Both Monro and his son Henry appear compulsively busy, Monro always on the move, Henry constantly drawing and working on projects. The year 1809 seems to give good examples, with the doctor at the height of his career. In January, Tom records that Papa was going to Bushey but did not on account of his pain, which was perhaps a foretaste of future problems that Monro had both with his legs and with stomach pains. Mama also was unwell, and did not go to dinner with Mr. Soane (later Sir John - architect and collector). John Constable came to dinner on January 14th, with William Alexander. Although older than Henry Monro, Constable was a steady friend to him in times of crisis, and they were both students at that time at the Academy Schools, in spite of Constable being considerably older. On March 5th of 1810, when he had decided to join the army, Henry called on Constable, and talked to him on the "army subject. Learnt particulars about the army" Henry wrote in his diary:'Had very deep thoughts about the Army. Settled that I would go into the

Army.' Presumably Constable had not been persuasive. Finally Henry made up his mind to continue at the Academy, and by April 14th he had decided, with help from his father. 'Papa settled I should continue painting.' The family had been reluctant to let Henry continue because they felt an artist's life was not a fitting one for a gentleman. That same summer Henry showed his first symptoms of ill health, and in fact was so seriously ill that the Monros called in Dr. Abernathy, the famous lecturer on anatomy. Meanwhile Henry's rich and influential cousins, the Culling Smiths offered to procure him a post in a government office, but he refused this too. Having recovered from his illness, in August, 1811, he set off on the Eclipse coach from St. Albans for a tour of Scotland. Unfortunately he became very ill again, so Tom and his cousin Fred were sent to bring him home, and he seems to have made a good recovery at that time.

The Monro gathering of young artists on a Friday night seems to have continued through the years 1806 and 1807, when Tom first began his diary, but these evenings were not frequent. It seems to have become more a gathering of former students, revived when there was a need. In January, 1806, Tom records that Linnell, Hunt and Turner came to draw. In April Mr. Sheppard 'drew in the evening and Mr. W. Smith was there'. Again in November, Linnel, Hunt and Turner came to draw, Tom records. Turner, beginning to work on his *Liber Studiorum* around this time, may have come to make use of the printing press at Adelphi Terrace. This was used to run off the outlines, drawn by Girtin, Turner and Hearne, also Edridge and Henderson, and used by the young students for the purpose of colouring in, in order to learn the skills of shading. Outlines by J.R. Cozens were also used, leading to some mystery as to what was in the collection of this artist, and came with him to Monro's house. Turner does not seem to have been a particular friend to the Monro children, but he did visit Tom at Oxford in

May, 1807, and on 15th he and Henry 'went into the water together.' By 25th May, Turner, back in London, dined with the Monros, along with Hoppner, Edridge and Alexander. We know that Hunt was a good friend of the Monro boys, also Peter de Wint, both at one time students, but both family friends also, and guests on more than one occasion at Bushey. William Hunt's mother was on calling terms with the Monro family, and is recorded by Tom as having a daughter. Roget mentions that Hunt "often stayed with the good Doctor for a month at a time, and was paid by him 7/6d a day for the drawings he produced". Roget continued:" He drew for Dr. Monro an interior of St. Albans Abbey Church, about Bushey and in the woodlands of Cassiobury. Wm. Hunt used to be trundled on a sort of barrow with a hood over it...It is said that Dr. Monro not only bought what he drew, but superintended the production, and was "wont to sponge out the parts that displeased him."[1]

In July, 1809, Henry started work on his portrait of his father, now hanging in the Royal College of Physicians. Joseph Farington also came to visit the family at Bushey, and this visit is recorded in detail in his diary, so that again one can see how the time was passed in walking and sketching, and being entertained by Sally at the piano in the evening. She was described by Farington as being a good player, who also sang very well. He described her hands, with enlarged knuckles, from having played too much on the piano when she was young. The circle was almost complete since Hearne and Edridge were also guests at this time. They all went to Cassiobury on 5th July, and Edridge made a portrait of Hearne. The visit lasted for four days, and Farington left on 7th July. Later that month, on 28th July, Mama, Sally, Sophy and Papa were recorded as dining at Cassiobury, along with Mr. Eden and Turner. The dinner was disturbed by Mr. Capel, a neighbour, coming by to deliver a note to Monro from Dr. Pemberton, who was one of the doctors in attendance on the King at that time, and Monro left. He did not return until 31st July, bringing Dr. Roberts, an old friend, who stayed for a couple of days, which might indicate that Monro was talking to him and discussing with him various aspects of the King's illness.

The beginning of October, 1809, Tom was still at Bushey, and on 6th John Laporte came to stay, whilst a neighbour Miss Capper, was invited for dinner, no doubt to help entertain him. There were several visits back and forth to Cassiobury, with a sale at Aldenham, noted for its beautiful garden, attended by Monro and Tom. Tom also noted that the Jubilee was celebrated on 25th October, being the 50th year of George Ill's reign. Having dined at Cassiobury on 2nd November, the following day Lord Essex and Mr. Turner called. Papa brought home a dog, which the boys christened Mallord Turner, and Tom adds the comment 'My Lord'. Did this indicate that the young family found Turner difficult, perhaps arrogant, as his manners may well have expressed a lordly attitude. Turner adopted towards Dr. Monro a patronising attitude, indicated by his purchase of his old drawings at the Monro sale, apparently with the intention of destroying them. Turner may have been ashamed of his early associations, although acknowledging the benefit to his career, but he did not go out of his way to continue the friendship in later years.

An extraordinary adventure began, when Henry, with' Papa' and Tom went to the City to fit Henry out prior to his joining the navy. This he did on 6th January, 1812, when he boarded the frigate 'Amelia' at Gravesend. By the 18th January, his brother recorded that Henry arrived from Yarmouth, having had leave to quit the navy, which had made him miserable. Henry seems to have found the navy, in the middle of January, a much less exciting affair than may have been suggested by the exploits of Nelson. It does seem strangely indulgent of his father to have even allowed him to undertake such a thing, but rather than exasperation at his son's exploits, he seems to have had other things on his mind. Tom records that he had spent time with Tom Snow - the banker, whilst Elborough called again, Monro's brother-in-law, also Uncle Charles. No further details are given by Tom, but there is evidence to suggest that financial concerns were playing some part in the affairs of Monro. Tom and Henry spent the 31st January on a social round of visits, calling on the Coxs' of the Foundling Hospital, the Goulds, the Charles Monro family and Hoppner and his son. Henry was at work on a portrait of his Uncle Charles by February, and also drawing the portrait of Sir Joshua Reynolds, and Sir Culling Smith. Probably no other painter at this time has left such a detailed account as Henry did, of what he painted from day to day, almost from hour to hour. He painted Tom's portrait several times, also his cousins, especially Julia and then Fanny. He made many sketches for Lord Essex, who obviously took great interest in his work. By March, 1810, Henry had his own rooms at Vinsons, who had a picture framing business at Covent Garden From this record we can see for examples that on 28th February, 1811, "Drew my father as large as nature in his doctor's gown. Finished March 8th."[2] From casual extracts of his own diary it would seem that whilst Henry was greatly beloved by his family, his impulsive disposition and a certain wilfulness caused unpleasant scenes. His father complained to him of his behaviour towards his mother, but most of Henry's 'rows' with his father appear to be over his extravagance on clothes. An example of one or two purchases from his diary gives an indication:

1810
Nov.5th Ordered new black coat – Hunter – pair of brown leather pantaloons, Davies
Nov. 8 Papa talking about money affairs, alteration in my conduct etc.

Nov. 11 Put on black and brown leathers for the first time
         forPrincessAmelia
Nov. 19 Ordered new pair of breeches, Davies
1811
Feb. 10 Pa spoke to me about Brown's bill
         and about bills in general
Feb. 12 Went to Hunters and was measured for new white
         waistcoat
April 4 Went to Hunters and ordered new waistcoat.
         May 1st Ordered new blue coat
         May 7 Ordered new pair of chocolate pantaloons
         May 8 To Hunters and ordered new waistcoat.

There is a record of his paying Hunter £50, and afterwards
he appears to have gone to a man called Finlayson for his
waistcoats, which he took to ordering two and even three at
a time. It is impossible not to be surprised at Dr. Monro's
annoyance at his son's extravagance, but the genuine
affection which existed between them was proved during
Monro's serious illness in 1812. It was Henry who was in
constant attendance upon his father from the middle of April
to the middle of May, when there is an entry on May 14th:
"My father very considerably better. Gave me the Watteaus
in memory of attention during his illness." These may have
been engravings after Watteau, but what became of them is
not known, as they do not appear in the catalogue of the sale
of prints which took place on the death of Dr. Thomas.

Henry and Tom went frequently to the theatre. The new
Covent Garden Theatre had just re-opened, when some of
the family went to a play there 'for half price', in September
1809. The play was called *The Same Riot.* Tom records he
saw Kemble in Hamlet and 'was much delighted', and saw
him also in *Penindack,* besides visiting with Henry the
Lyceum Theatre. Tom himself was overwhelmed when on
25th February, 1809, the Drury Lane Theatre burnt down,
and he spent all the next day, with Henry, looking at the

ruins and recording on 27th, that he saw part of the remaining wall taken down. For Tom, who was serious and hard working, the theatre was obviously his great escape from reality, and he went frequently, so that this event was a very great tragedy in his life, when he was still very young. He seems to constantly refer to it in his diary, and was again there looking at the ruins with his mother on 3rd March. This interest was to stay with Tom all of his recorded life, and in 1815 he went to see Kemble in April in the newly rebuilt Drury Lane Theatre in *Stranger*. By 18th May he wrote in his diary that he had made a list of all the characters he had seen Kemble play, whilst his new wife Sarah was at the Walker's party, and then by 21st of that month Kemble was dead. Kemble and Kean, who had just had a benefit playing *Henry VI*, were frequently mentioned by Tom, who along with his father, attended the theatre at frequent intervals. Edmund Kean made his first appearance at Drury Lane in 1814 as Shylock to great success.

There seems little doubt that the theatre affected artists of the period deeply, introducing not only dramatic scenery, but also lighting, conveying very graphically some of the current ideas on the picturesque, and introducing the excitement of moonlit and night scenes. Gainsborough carried out numerous experiments, and opened doors for Turner as a result, and Turner referred to this in his Lectures, given at the Royal Academy. Turner seems to have been involved briefly as well, and was probably the artist responsible for the panorama for the *Battle of the Nile* in 1799, advertised in *The True Briton* on 13th June.[3] Turner, always curious about all forms of landscape, seems to have been stirred out of his usual approach in order to conceive, design and organise the panorama himself. Ker Porter was involved with the *Eruption of Mount Vesuvius* at about the same time, and this show closed in 1800. Panoramas used a transparent screen, which could be moved, but this could also reveal dramatic lighting effects. Girtin exhibited his

Eidometropolis in 1802, months before he died, on view at the Spring Gardens to great acclaim, and was intending to do the same for Paris, having prepared so many drawings. The idea was based on de Loutherbourg's *Eidophusikon,* first displayed in 1781. Girtin was treated by Dr. Monro before he so tragically died on 9th November. Three days after he died his London panorama reopened for the benefit of his widow Mary Ann, and their young son, indicating how popular the idea of moving scenery was, as exhibited by the panorama, although it is not recorded that much money was raised for his widow. Shortly after this some twenty of his views of Paris were published, the outlines having been etched by the artist, whilst the effects were 'slightly' added, (a pale wash presumably) in aquatint, copied from Girtin's original drawings. It was after Girtin's funeral at St. Pauls, Covent Garden, that Turner made his famous tribute.

It appears that Dr. Monro acquired Gainsborough's light box from his daughter, although Thomas Lawrence, the artist and portrait painter, wanted to buy this, and had been asked for one hundred guineas, but no record is given of why Monro was chosen, beyond the fact that he was a family friend, nor is there any record of the transaction. The box was inspired by the *Eidophusikon,* which consisted of a small stage some eight feet wide, and about six feet high, on which moving scenes made up of painted flaps and transparencies, were shown to small audiences. The whole thing moved mechanically and was accompanied by music. Gainsborough's transparencies were developed on a smaller scale inspired by the idea. Displayed in a box, lit from behind by the artist, with candles, various scenes were painted on "transparencies", which were glass, and were to be of enormous influence on his later work. Gainsborough, like the artists in watercolour, was keenly aware that landscapes needed to be boldly painted to attract attention on the crowded walls of the Royal Academy. The idea of trying to create an inner light was achieved in his case by glazes. Painted glass transparencies were lit from behind by candlelight filtered through a silk screen. The artist created a small stage setting, into which he could then fit a suitable rural scene, such as some of his 'cottage' subjects, so he could paint from his studio, creating a foreground with gravel and using broccoli to simulate the trees. A candle gave brilliant effects of light and deep shade, as in his *Wooded Landscape with Cattle by a Pool, 1782.*[4] This light box was recorded by Tom as being used to entertain family guests early in January, 1811, and it seems to have been brought out on many occasions. It must have been in the family by 3rd March, 1810, when Tom records that Sir William Beechey dined (this must have been shortly after his knighthood), along with Mr. Hearne, Edridge and Alexander, also Uncle Charles and his Aunt Jane Monro. The next day he writes, "Homewards with Henry and James Earle, seeing Gainsborough Show", indicating that at this time it was a new toy, and so displayed for company entertainment, and remained popular with them for some time, according to Tom. The family would play music, since we know there was a piano in the house, and sing, obviously inventing imaginary stories around the various scenes.

The Monro family gave a dance on January 18th, 1811. It seems not to have been a special event as far as Tom was concerned, but more can be learned from an entry made by the doctor himself, in the brief diary that he seems to have begun that year, and then put away. Monro wrote: "I spent this day at my brother's house in Chandos Street with my family, where there were nearly thirty Monros of the family collected. A dance in the evening. One cousin, Charles Culling Smith was expected, but did not come as prophesied the day before by CM. (Charles Monro- his brother). His connexions in life seem to have raised him so much above our level, that it is ridiculous to expect more from him than expressions of civility at a casual meeting. If he were inclined to keep up any friendly society with us his first cousins, the way of so doing would not be difficult. Mr. Seton was at the party. I much lament that I never was acquainted with this gentleman before last winter -1 think him a very pleasant agreeable man full of anecdote and with manners just suited to my ideas of a friend and companion." [6] Thomas Monro was related to the Culling Smiths through his mother, whilst Hoppner painted a conversation piece of Mrs. Culling Smith and her family.

Monro also wrote at this time: "I think without prejudice that my daughter was the best dancer in the room. There seems to be a sort of native ease and grace in her movements which are captivating and well calculated to attract admiration. I did not quit the scene till half past one o'clock in the morning and slept well tho' I ate supper contrary to my usual practice." We know from various descriptions that Sally was musical, and as recorded by Farrington could play and sing 'with much skill', since she entertained him when he visited Bushey in July, 1809. On 5th July, they drank tea at nine o'clock, whilst listening to Sally and her father, also Edridge, who all sang to entertain the guests, as recorded by Farington.

Tom by this time had finished at Oxford and begun to attend Dr. Abernethy's lectures in preparation for his further degree in medicine. Both Tom and Sally were concerned with a particular person in their lives, in Tom's case Sarah Cox, who he told his father he fell in love with at Uncle Charles' Christmas party. Her father was Samuel Compton Cox, Governor of the Foundling Hospital, also its Treasurer by 1798. Sally Monro began to see a great deal more of Henry Earle, the son of a doctor, and his family. Sir J. Earle and Lady Earle and their son Edward, were also friends of the Monro family. Henry was training to be a doctor. By September of 1814, Tom mentions that Henry Earle spoke to his father about Sally. His advances seem to have been acceptable at this stage, and he then seems to be continually involved in family activities, although no mention is made of an engagement. He was a frequent theatre companion to the boys, but Sally seems not to have been included. It was much more difficult for ladies to attend the theatre unless a box was taken for the evening, since they could not stand in the pit with the general crowds, as this would not have been socially acceptable for a young respectable girl. Meanwhile Tom and Henry Earle were off to see Kemble in Corialanus, Kean in Macbeth, although one evening both Tom and Sarah and Henry Earle and Sally did go to the new Drury Lane, in a box, with the doctor.

In 1815 Sally appears to have had a set-back described in a letter from her father on June 20th as the "trying circumstance of the present moment." A true Highland Scot he wastes no words, nor does he leave her in any doubt of his own devotion and sympathy, as he gives her wise advice. "In these trying circumstances you will as well as you can keep your mind in an equal and quiet state and that your friends at Woodhill will allow you to stay a short time till the storm of contending feelings has a little subsided." Her engagement to Henry Earle seems to have been broken off, as Thomas Monro goes on to say that Henry Earle has written her a letter which he, her father, thinks "had better not be sent for a day or two". He had no doubt exercised the privilege of parents in those days of reading it. He then finishes the letter by saying "Perhaps your visit had better terminate with the present week, as I know not how your Mama can support herself so much alone as she is, for any longer period and with so much on her mind respecting this business." Tom merely wrote in his diary:"Heard of Sally having discarded Henry Earle." As a brother he then goes onto a more important subject "Heard of a great battle at Waterloo on 18th". It appears that the broken engagement had to do with Sally's religious feelings. She became a Methodist, at a time when feelings were running high, and there was a revival of Wesleyanism, although her father was outspoken on his dislike of their particular madness. The family went quite often to the Percy Chapel, especially Tom, and a popular preacher was Mr. Noel. Tom subsequently persuaded Mr. Noel to visit Sally on several occasions, but she did not change her mind. Sally seems to have fallen under some religious fervour and felt that she could not marry Henry Earle. Writing from Berners Street, in an undated letter, Henry Earle sent back Sally's portrait by Henry Monro, "my much esteemed and ever regretted friend Henry". He found it too painful to regard with pleasure, he wrote. He refers to this "unhappy business, and goes on to entreat Dr. Monro "not to evince any displeasure towards Miss Monro, who I am sure must require the kindness and support of her family. I have already made my father acquainted with the termination of the contract and have assigned as a reason his dislike of early marriages. I could not think of any other mode of explaining your daughter's conduct." What that conduct was is not explained but it does appear that the action was Sally's, and not that of Henry Earle, who remained a family friend, especially to Tom, as he went on to successfully become a doctor.

By 1813 Tom had begun to see the occasional patient, and to do the rounds with his father. This was just as well as that year Monro had not been well and had to see Dr. Baillie several times. Tom took his medical degree in 1814, an M.A. at Oxford, and as the family circumstances began to change, it was only a short period before he succeeded his father as Physician at Bethlem Hospital after the House of Commons enquiry, and the subsequent events. Tom also took over the private 'mad-house' at Brook House, Hackney, and also some responsibilities at Brompton Hospital, initially through Monro's patronage, but later his father-in-law who was also connected there, showed an interest in Tom's progress. He became an FRCP in 1817, also a Censor of the Royal College of Physicians in 1816, 1819, 1829 and again in 1837. Tom was also Harveian Orator in 1834, and Treasurer of the College from 1845 to 1856. He had had plenty of experience travelling with his father to all his institutions and seems to have taken on the responsibility without question. He married Sarah Cox, on 14th April, 1814, and they moved to No. 16 Gower Street, which Tom had acquired the year before, and spent time furnishing, finally proudly recording in his diary that his name had been put upon the door in September, 1813. Their son Edward was born in January, 1815. It appeared to be a very happy marriage, and they had many children, including a son Henry, who eventually became a doctor and took on the responsibilities at Bethlem Hospital. He was also artistic. Tom continued to keep up his diary, and the young couple led a very social life, full of dinner parties, visits to the theatre, and musical evenings, not to mention three nights of 'Illuminations', following Napoleon's defeat at Waterloo.

Henry Monro, Tom's brother, also left a diary, begun in May 1811, and from it one can see that he was greatly loved by his family, but that his impulsive disposition caused family rows[7]. He records that he "had a terrible quarrel with Madam", and even "row with Tom about lending money", also "Papa mentioned about behaving to my mother", and then again a few days later "Had a tantrum bobus with my mother, and further "the last of all rows with Ally and my mother etc. - my mother in histericks." Ally refers to his young brother Alexander, and Henry often argued with his mother about her treatment of his two small brothers, since she was apparently both weak and foolish, and could not stand up to them. Henry was also very extravagant, as his frequent descriptions of visits to various tailors indicate, and that no doubt was a cause of family friction. On November 4th, 1811, "Papa called at my rooms for the 1st time this year." In September of the previous year

Henry had moved his painting room away from the top floor of the house at Adelphi Terrace, to a room in Covent Garden. From the records he seemed to continue living both at home and at Vinsons, but with a separate studio, where his friends frequently visited him

Henry's diaries were largely concerned with his drawing and painting, but they are also full of references to his feelings, his love for his cousin Julia, and his efforts at self improvement. His sprawling, often almost illegible handwriting and his very bad spelling can be attributed to his short schooling, but this did not deter him from extensive writing. Not only did he keep a daily diary from April, 1808, to within a few days of his death on March 5th, 1814, but in 1810 he began to write 'An Abridged History of England'. He worked for this for many months for two hours each day, and in 1811 began to write his 'life'. Neither of these has survived. He was full of fun and high spirits, and at other moments filled with despair. Tom, who referred to him as 'poor Henry' packed his clothes when he was going away, gave him little tips of money, read to him and generally looked after him. They went everywhere together. Henry was a popular student at the Academy Schools, and both young and older artists seem to have been attracted to him. He mentions Fuseli, Sir Anthony Carlisle, Sir William Beechy, whose son was a friend. He certainly called on Sir George Beaumont on several occasions. Constable and Haydon were friends, as were Lascelles Hoppner, Kirkup, probably his greatest friend, and also Eastlake and Dighton. He knew J.M.W. Turner, but does not appear to have liked him. Henry was very active at the Academy Schools and was made the 'President' of the students. His progress was rapid, and in 1811 he exhibited at the R.A for the first time. Five drawings were accepted, including his portraits of his father's friend Dr. Roberts, Uncle Charles and one of his father. The other two subjects were *Boys Laughing and Boys at Marbles*. His work other than that in crayon or pencil, was in oils, but after 1812, mostly in pen and indian ink, often on stained or 'coffeed' paper. In 1812 he exhibited at the R.A. a fine self-portrait in oil, which shows him to be dark-eyed, solemn and slim, with a suggestion of a flicker of humour about his month.[8] In 1813 he had attempted a more ambitious work of *Iago and Desdemona,* and the next year he was awarded posthumously a Premium of 100 guineas by the British Institution for the painting *The Death of Wolsey.* This was later sold by his father to cover his debts.[9]

The death of Henry on 5th March, 1814, was a sad blow to all the family, but especially to his brother Tom. When he died he left considerable debts, some re-paid by Tom, but other had to be settled by the sale of his pictures. Early in February Henry had caught a cough, which Tom also had, and Dr. Roberts had to be sent for as he was very unwell. By the 20th he was in bed, very ill and spitting blood, all recorded by Tom. Tom sat up with him on many nights, as did Henry Earle, showing an extraordinary depth of devotion, whilst both Dr. Roberts and Dr. Pemberton came to visit, and bled him. They must have applied blisters as well, since Henry Earl is reported as having dressed these, since Tom was off by day on his doctoring duties. There is no mention of Henry's mother being in attendance. The end when it came was swift, and on 5th March Henry died at twenty minutes to ten in the evening. Poor Tom described the following day as ' the most melancholy day', when his Uncle Charles fetched John and Alexander from Harrow. Bob was by this time at Oxford. Henry was buried at Bushey on Friday, March 11th, and almost immediately Tom records that his room was "turned out" and that he took many of his books and drawings to Gower Street. Henry Earl was by then very unwell, so it may well have been a severe strain of influenza that had affected Henry.

Henry was the outgoing member of the family, friend to all his brothers, and very involved with his artistic career, always drawing or creating. He was extravagant, especially with his clothes, and his diary is full of descriptions of a new waistcoat, expensive boots, or other clothes he had purchased. Tom meanwhile was much more studious, but also steady and dependable, taking responsibility for many household chores, such as 'cleaning the lustres', cleaning silver, and taking care of his father's books, for example taking his collection of Walter Scott novels to the bookbinder. He refers constantly to the books he was reading, and was the one always cleaning or sorting his father's books. There is evidence to show that Monro had a considerable collection, and some new and perhaps controversial art books. Turner went through a period of drawing from 'blots', splattered on his paper, as did Girtin. This idea was inspired initially perhaps by Alexander Cozens, father to John Robert, whose work was so admired by Monro. We know that his son took up with the idea briefly, and this had been written about in a book, published in 1785, entitled *A New Method of Assisting the Invention in Drawing Original Compositions of Landscapes*. This seems to have been known to Uvedale Price, who refers to it in his Essays, and to Pyne the writer. Monro, with his interest in the Cozenses, would almost certainly have had a copy, and he had some of the senior Cozens' work having bought this at a sale in 1781. It may well be that Turner would have read this work from Monro's library, as he was certainly influenced by its ideas. Tom and his father had dinner with Uvedale Price in August, 1811. This was also the time when Monro took his two eldest boys and revisited Fetcham, staying at the Swan in Leatherhead. It was obviously a visit to see old friends, since the boys rode over to see William Locke with their father, who lived at Norbury Park, and then dined at Mr. Carter's house before returning to London. It is the only time that Tom recorded such a visit. The Locke's house was new, and was in the height of fashion, situated on a hill above the Dorking gap. It was known for its painted room, whose walls were decorated with landscapes in *trompe d'oeuil* fashion to blend with the real landscape outside, so giving an illusion of being in the open air. Locke was a direct descendant of John Locke the philosopher, who believed that knowledge comes directly from Nature, and that no art is superior to Nature. If William shared these views, it is understandable that he and Monro were friends.'10

An entry in the doctor's brief diary for 1811, written in January, mentions: "I have been reflecting today upon the multitude of bills I have got to pay - where I shall find money to settle them I know not. I have generally beforehand had money at my Bankers, but my house at Bushey has cost me so much money and my family is so much more expensive, that I presume I am distressed on that account."[11] We know from Tom's diary that by 1815 Monro had been called to appear before a Committee of the House of Commons. He had also had meetings with his brother, who had become worried concerning the business side of Brook House, and also about the finances of Bedlam. This could be one of the reasons that Tom refers often to the visits of Mr. Paul. This would have been Paul Colnaghi, who was employed by the Prince Regent to obtain a number of prints and drawings by Paul Sandby and others of the English School to add to the Royal collection, which was later transferred to Windsor. By 1799 Colnaghi had moved to 23 Cockspur Street, which became a social rendezvous for the upper few thousand of Society. He gathered together members of Society at 3 o'clock levees, where English Marchionesses, Foreign Princes, Knights, Dames and gentlemen met as if at a Club. Levees were also held at Carleton House. These were held once a month during the Season, and again seem to have been an occasion when everyone in town paraded in their best clothes around one of the large over furnished rooms at the Prince of Wales's residence, Carlton House, to find out who else was in town. Tom and Henry went there on 10th February, 1810, where they met Mr. Angerstein, and then went to see his collection of pictures. Sir George Beaumont was closely involved with the arrangements when the Angerstein collection was left to the Nation, forming an important nucleus for the National Gallery Collection, but then known as The British Galleries. Dr. Monro and Tom were again at a Levee in 1812. Paul Colnaghi and his son Dominic were early to appreciate the work of Constable, and assisted him in his publication of his *English Landscape* series of mezzotints, engraved by Lucas. It seems therefore, very likely that Colnaghi may have been interested in some of the drawings held by Monro.

On 28th July, 1811, Tom records that" Dr. Pemberton sent a note for Papa", which seems to be an indication that Monro was again consulted about George III. Monro went to dine with Pemberton on 31st July, in Windsor, and returned with his friend Dr. Roberts the following day, who Monro may have brought with him from London, to advise him on the consultation. Dr. and Mrs. Pemberton came to Bushey on 24th September, and the Reverend and Mrs. Vivian were invited to dinner. It seems to have been the beginning of a friendship that was to last for many years between the Pembertons and the Monros. Thomas was sent for by the Queen for consultation three times in October, at least four times in November, and again in December. Early the following year he went to Windsor to dine with Dr. Latham. The King's illness was to give him a fascinating interlude in a life that was so soon to become beset with problems. Meanwhile from Tom's diary it is possible to trace how he gradually took on more of his father's work, whilst still visiting the Adelphi almost every other day, not only assisting his father professionally, but also concerning himself with his younger brothers. Bob appears to have been at Oxford through the years 1815 to 1819. Jack was giving a good deal of trouble, once staying out all night, so Tom was called in to cope with the situation. His parents by this time were spending more and more time at Bushey, usually accompanied by Sally and young Alexander, who was 16 years old on 14th June, 1818. He went to Oxford with his father to see Bob graduate in May, 1819, with his Batchelor's degree, as recorded by Tom, who does not say in what subject. He also records that Jack received a medal at the Arts & Sciences, so gradually the family were growing up, as the Doctor's health began to give him trouble, which is why perhaps he decided to have a change and take his younger boys on a tour around the country.

1. Roget - *History of the Old Watercolour Society* .pp77-9 Vol. 1
2. In family collection. Copy with the author. Last recording made in Dec. 1813.
3. Lindsay, Jack -*Tamer* Granada Books 1973 p89 Lindsay gives other details, and indicates that in 1799 Turner's mother came under Monro's care.
4. This picture is now in Gainsborough's house at Sudbury, Suffolk.
5. The box is now in the V&A, and was sold at Monro's sale at Christies in 1833.
6. Taken from a typed record of a diary once in the possession of Mrs. Coode*, and then her son, Rev. Foxley Norris.
7. Copy of Henry's diary is in the possession of the family of Dr. Jeferiss. The original was made available in 1922 to F. How, who wrote a book on *Thomas Monro & His Circle,* but never published it. The original document has since disappeared.
8. Henry's portrait now in the Monro family. Private Collection
9. This portrait was bought by Dr. Jeferiss some thirty years ago. Private Collection
10. Harman, Claire *Fanny Burney* Harper Collins, London 2000 pi88
11. From a typed record of a diary once in possession of Mrs. Coode, and then her son Rev. Foxley Norris.

CHAPTER 7 - THE KING'S MALADY

As recorded, Dr. Monro was called in to advise on the stateof George Ill's health. In addition to all that has come down in tradition regarding the treatment of the King, there are the constant references in Tom Monro's diaries to his father going to Windsor, and on occasion he himself going with him. The main agent in calling in Dr. Monro was the Queen, through the Lord Chancellor and others. It was also the Queen, who with gracious tact dismissed Monro when she found the position to be impossible, according to members of the Court, owing to the presence of Dr. Willis and his son. The Queen said that the condition of George lll was such that whoever was advising on his treatment must be constantly in attendance, and that she could not countenance that anyone who was doing such important work for so many, should be called away for one person, even the King. This was of course a great tribute to the work by Monro at Bedlam as well as with a number of his private patients. If she had not had a great opinion of the skill of Monro she would hardly have taken the initial step in summoning him.

As early as 1765, Sir George Baker was summoned to attend the King, and recorded in his diary the details of his visit. "In the afternoon (22nd October, 1765) I was received by His Majesty in a very unusual manner, of which I had not the least expectation. The look of his eyes, the tone of his voice, every gesture and his whole deportment represented a person in a most furious passion of anger. One medicine had been too powerful, another had only teased him without effect. The importation of senna ought to be prohibited, and he would give orders that in future it should never be given to the royal family. With frequent repetition of this and similar language, he detained me three hours. His pulse was much quickened, but I did not number the strokes. Having no opportunity of speaking to the Queen, I wrote a note to Mr. Pitt immediately on my return to town, and informed him that I had just left the King in an agitation of spirits nearly bordering upon delirium. Mr. Pitt called on me that evening, and I had an opportunity of giving him a full description of His Majesty's condition"[1] This seems to have been a short attack, and the King made a full recovery. The King had another attack in November, 1788, and again seems to have made a full recovery, but not before John Monro was called as a consultant.

In 1794 Dr. Fordyce made an 'estimate of symptoms and appearances,' when the King appears to have had another attack. After a short summary of his examination the doctor listened to the patient's complaints but royal protocol prevented the doctor from enquiring of the King about his symptoms. If not addressed first, royal physicians could not ask questions. Again the King made a recovery, although he seems to have been aware of the seriousness of the attack since in 1795 he requested Parliament to make provision for a regency in case 'it should please God to put a period to my life whilst my successor is of tender years.' In 1801 he confided to the Rev. John Willis "I do feel very ill. I am much weaker than I was -1 have prayed to God all night that I might die or that he will spare my reason should it be otherwise -for God's sake keep it from your father(Dr. Francis Willis) and his friend." (Richard Hurd, Bishop of Worcester) Willis, the father, was a colourful figure, an Anglican clergyman, who took up the care and cure of the insane, running a private madhouse at Greatford in Lincolnshire, that specialised in affluent patients. Like other progressive doctors of the insane Francis Willis had faith in occupational therapy and the value of kindness, reason and a civilized atmosphere. However as his treatment of the King was later to indicate, he also believed that threats, force and fear were sometimes indispensable weapons in the doctor's armoury. In his diary for 1788, he had obviously had the King in some form of straight jacket. On 24th December he recorded: 'The waistcoat was taken off at nine - & blisters dress'd- discharg'd well - very sore- Pulse 96 - perspir'd through the night profusely - but little sleep.'[2] The crisis occurred in 1788 when the fifty year old George lll went mad. The so called 'mad doctors' at that period were thus referred to in Parliament and were called in to take charge of the King. Amongst them were not only Dr. Willis and his son, but also Dr. John Monro, father of Thomas. A bulletin issued at the time, 'Spring 1788', announced that 'The king's health is giving anxiety. It was suggested that Dr. John Monro, physician to Bedlam Hospital, be called into consultation. Dr. Warren, to prove the King incurable wrote to Dr. Monro on 18th January, 1789:

> "Can you tell me without much trouble what you consider the symptom or symptoms of incurability."
>
> Yours mst. affectionately,   R. Warren Sackville Street

Hannah Woodcock (Thomas's wife) signed a note on this letter to the effect that "Dr. Warren wrote the enclosed to my father (in-law). The answer is in my Mother's hand, "(again meaning her mother-in law). It had obviously been treasured in the family archives.[3]   In a letter of reply Dr. John had replied:

> "I should look upon that insanity as likely to prove incurable which comes on towards the middle stage of life without any known cause to which it can be attributed unless it be a family complaint. The symptoms are great deprivation of sense, tendency to fatuity: every tendency to that disposition is to be dreaded where the disorder is not abated by medicine or management: when there is a want of natural sleep." [4]
>
> John Monro   Bedford Square

135

An article appeared in the Morning Chronicle on 28th November, 1788 declaring 'Disorder has deranged the head - it is not a mental incapacity called "insanity", but changeability from confusion, excitement to insight and composure somewhat between insanity and delirium.' Supporters of the delirium theory were disheartened and then all theories were confounded by the King's swift and complete return to clarity and reason. Physicians were evasive, and only two took a definite stand, both having political motives for their views. Dr. Richard Warren, a Whig sympathiser, also physician to the Prince of Wales, pronounced danger to life in 1788. The Rev. Dr. Francis Willis (Tory) was brought down from Lincolnshire with his son, by Pitt, who told Parliament in 1788 that there were great hopes of His Majesty's recovery. The Willis's implied diagnosis was delirium and derangement with fever. Dr. Anthony Addington, who looked after Lord Chatham, was hopeful that it was not mania, because it had not for its forerunner the usual melancholy. The King's surgeon, John Hunter, thought it to be systemic affection. A number of other opinions and surmises are mentioned, but do not bear on the visits of Dr. Monro. [5] In 1789 the Prime Minister reported that the state of His Majesty's health does not render His Majesty (incapable) either of coming to Parliament or of attending to public business. After the crisis in 1788 twelve years elapsed in which the King was relatively free from trouble.

At this point an excellent description by Roy Porter should be quoted in order to give further insight into the Madness Business. 'Two hundred and fifty years ago, our forebears, doctors and lay people alike, would have found little difficulty in identifying a madman. Some victims were overactive, violent, frenzied, dangerous; others were withdrawn, depressed, suicidal even. So there were maniacs and there were melancholies, and intelligent observers had even grasped that both these conditions could appear in turn in the same individual, though the term manic-depressive was a much later coinage. There was no agreement as to what caused this terrible affliction that reduced humans to the level of beasts or helpless infants.'

The Scientific Revolution and the Age of Reason cast doubts on all this. The idea of possession, it was now argued, was itself a delusion. Most Georgian physicians therefore opted for a physical explanation. Like other diseases, insanity was the result of some defect in the body. Old style doctors blamed the humours; mania arose from too much yellow bile, or choler, despondency from excess of black bile (or melancholia). Some doctors blamed the guts, or more fashionable still, the nervous system, if nerves were fibres in a state of tension, obviously people were 'stressed' or too highly strung. George lll used to insist that he was 'nervous'. In the end however, what caused madness seemed to matter less than how it should be treated.

New social and economic opportunities in the eighteenth century were important in shaping the whole range of medical practice under George III. William Hunter, who won fame and fortune out of his anatomy school, also William Battie, M.D. F.R.S., pioneer psychiatrist and founder of St. Luke's, a private lunatic asylum, made huge profits. They demonstrated that others besides quacks were involved in the commercial developments of medicine. Battie, who was the son of the Vicar of Modbury, in Devon, was the doctor who caused Thomas Monro's father John, to write a paper renouncing his particular methods for the care of the insane. However under the Monros at Bethlem, students and physicians were refused permission to study patients until 1843, whilst at St. Luke's the first attempts to instruct by actual observation of the phenomenon of madness took place under Dr. Battie.

At this time there was a three-tiered hierarchy at the College of Physicians, with the incorporation of the Surgeons and Apothecaries Companies. In terms of individual practitioners, the University educated physic tended to practise medicine as a liberal science, whilst the surgeon, who had trained by apprenticeship or increasingly at Edinburgh University, practiced a manual craft learned more by a hands-on experience. Lastly there was the Apothecary, who kept the shop, or was the man on the scene, as was Mr. Haslam, working with Thomas Monro at Bedlam, but attending patients on a day to day basis, and deciding which of the many should receive the attention of Monro on his visits.

In 1763 the House of Commons Committee for inquiring into the state of private mad-houses in the Kingdom was formed. Two physicians 'distinguished by their knowledge and their practice in cases of lunacy' were called to give evidence, namely Dr. Battie and Dr. John Monro. It was resolved at that time, by the authority, opinions and experience of these two physicians, and by the confessions of persons keeping private mad-houses, "that the present state of the private madhouses in the Kingdom requires the interposition of the legislature." It would seem that the madness of the King, had brought the whole matter into the public eye once again by 1816, since there was no doubt that grave abuses were still taking place in the treatment of the insane at this time.

In 1788 and 1789 Sir George Baker and Dr. Reynolds treated the King in Kew House, also Sir Lucas Pepys. It was stated at that time that 'it appeared that the Blister on His Leg and the Musk and Bark he now takes quantities of have been of infinite service.' The King appeared to make a complete recovery at this time. All however, was not so harmonious when Dr. Willis was brought on the scene. He reported that the King had not spoken a word of reason since his illness, whilst Sir George Baker was outraged that Dr. Willis permitted the Queen to see the King. Willis felt that if the King had a bad night following this, it was because of the blisters 'drawing on his legs', which were more likely to have disturbed him than having seen the Queen.[6]   Monro's approach seemed to have been more along the lines of his father's opinion, which was 'not to enquire into matters so far out of our reach as the causes of madness, but direct our knowledge to relieve them, leaving causes of this terrible calamity to such as can fancy there is any amusement in a disquisition of so unpleasant a nature.' When called in to see the King, he and Dr. Simpson seem to have spent many hours observing him, rather than actively treating him.

The charismatic Willis' forte was an intimidating technique of fixing patients with "the eye". This was not the method used by John Monro or his son Thomas, and was the reason why John Monro initially wrote his book, to cover Dr. Battie with ridicule. Like other progressive mad-doctors of the day, since the term psychiatrist was still a long way off, Willis had faith in occupational therapy, putting his patients to work on the grounds of his Lincolnshire estate as gardeners, 'threshers, thatchers, and other labourers, attired in black coats, white waistcoats, black silk breeches and stockings, and the head of each *bien poudree.'* The King's case helped overcome the conspiracy of silence traditionally surrounding lunacy, and prompted greater public concern for the humane treatment of the mentally ill in the nineteenth century, as Thomas Monro was to discover when he was called before the House of Commons, to answer to charges that he had been wanting in humanity towards the patients of Bedlam; a charge he was to prove unjustified.

Monro does seem to have run his own asylum with a less rigid system of control than Dr. Battie had done. Thomas Monro wrote the following observations when Evidence was taken before the House of Commons for regulating Madhouses in 1816. At Bethlem, he wrote:' the number of the objects to whom the charity is extended, and the comparative feebleness of the means for their relief, preclude the possibility of that nice discrimination, that minute and watchful attention to individual comfort, and those various indulgences that mitigate the sufferings of the disease, and the severity of indispensable restraint, which can only be gained from the anxious kindness of domestic affection, or commanded by the power of wealth.'[7]

Dr. Henry Monro once wrote of the special family tradition of "my grandfather being awakened one night when sleeping at his cottage at Bushey by a royal messenger summoning him to attend the King". A number of letters have been kept which if not actually corroborating this event, do at least bear witness to the fact that Thomas Monro was called into consultation. On May 13th, 1811, the following was written:-

> " Dr. Monro presents his most respectful compts. to the Lord Chancellor and begs leave to acknowledge the receipt of his Lordships very polite and condescending note as well as to express the due sense he feels of the Ld. Chancellors liberal -(obliterated) intentions. Dr. Monro takes the liberty of adding that in his opinion it is in vain to expect more effectual aid in this truly distressing case than is likely to ensue from the approved skill and experience of his Majesty's present Physicians."

This draft appears to have been a third effort to compose a perfectly correct letter. In all things Thomas Monro shows himself to be a perfectionist.

A letter marked Private addressed to Dr. Monro, Adelphi Terrace, Eldon and on the corner Rd. Aug. 12th, 1811, reads: -

Monday morning
"The Lord Chancellor presents his compliments to Dr. Monro and takes leave, by desire of the Council, assembled at Winds, such was the heroic approach favoured by all on Saturday, to inform him that under present circumstances it is not determined that there should be any change in the medical Attendance at Windsor. The Chancellor respectfully informs Dr. Monro that he will not fail to state to Mr. Perceval the extent of the Trouble which the Queens' Council have found themselves called upon to give Dr. Monro in requesting his advice."

The Council must have had under discussion the causes of madness. The great British philosopher, John Locke, suggested madness was deluded imagination, a kind of programming error in the software of the mind. Psychological accounts of this kind enjoyed a vogue in the new atmosphere of introspection and sensibility that characterized the Enlightment. The mad had long been neglected. Like Edgar in King Lear, lunatics had been allowed to wander. Only the lucky or unlucky few, ended up in London's Bethlem Hospital, or Bedlam, where they were reputedly kept near naked, often chained, sometimes beaten, (not in the days of Thomas Monro's tenure) and medicated only with bloodlettings, vomits and harsh purges. Bethlem may not in reality have been so brutal as its popular image and such treatments should not automatically be seen as expressions of a cruel disposition. There was method in them. Cold showers, straitjackets or restraining chairs, like the one Francis Willis used on the King, were intended to pacify patients, make them more tractable, and so amenable to reason. The great mid-eighteenth century physician William Battie came out in favour of "management" rather than "medicine". Moral management involved psychological close encounters between the physician and his charge, a battle of wills in which the doctor sought to master madness with a repertoire of persuasion, awe, will power, cunning, and all the force of personality at his disposal. Hypnotism ("Mesmerism") might occasionally be used.

Another letter, not dated, reads as follows: -

> "The Lord Chancellor has been ordered by Her Majesty to communicate to Dr. Monro her commands that he should attend to-morrow at two o'clock at Consultation of His Majesty's Physicians on the state of His Majesty's Health at Sir Henry Halford's in Curzon Street." Eldon

> Saturday morning.

This may have been the letter carried to Bushey by the Royal messenger referred to by Dr. Henry Monro.

The first mention of the King's case concerning Thomas Monro comes in Edward Thomas's diary on 4th August, 1811. He records in his diary that he went home to find a note from his father that he had been sent for by the Queen to consult about the King's illness. Tom received a packet after he was in bed. The next day Tom records that he wrote out 'The King's case'. His father then returned, called on Dr. Brydon in Red Lion Square, and then 'consulted with physicians'. He and his father then left London in a chaise, as far as Stanmore, where Monro dined, and Tom continued on to Merry Hill at Bushey on foot. Tom records that a carriage was sent for P. not saying if it was that night or the next day, and that by 6th August his father returned to tea. On the next day Tom records that he wrote out his father's answers about the King. Tom does not record any event, letter or message for August 12th.

However it may have been the answers, as written out by Tom, which caused the Lord Chancellor to refer to requesting the advice of Monro. This is further confirmed by another letter which begins:-

> "Sir: We have received the command of the Queens Council to hold a further consultation with you on the case submitted to you on the 4th August and we send you in the meantime what we believe to be an accurate representation of the Patients present condition in order to enable you to form a judgment upon it and to answer certain questions which Dr. Heberden is desirous to proposing to you.

> Windsor Castle   Henry Halford
> Sept. 17 1811   M.Baillie
>   W.Heberden
>   R Willis

The next consultation involving Dr. Thomas Monro seems to have been on 9th October, when he went to Windsor having instructed Tom to take his place at Bedlam. Tom also seems to have been given responsibilities at the private home Brook House, where he went on 12th October, to find a note from his father from Windsor, who finally returned on 14th October from there. We learn nothing from Tom's diary as to how much his father consulted with him, but it must have been a time when the King was very unstable, since Monro and Henry are recorded as having gone again to Windsor on 18th 'in a chair', which would have been a translation for a chaise, no doubt sent from Windsor Castle. This was a busy time also for Tom who recorded that he took his degree of Bachelor of Medicine on 24th October, in Oxford, to return the next day to find his father and Henry had returned from Windsor. Mr. Edridge, he records, came to tea that evening, tea being taken around 8 to 9 p.m., several hours after dinner, perhaps so the two good friends could discuss some of the events of the visit. On 18th November, Joseph Farington again leaves a good description in his diary of conversations that he must have had with Monro, giving further insight into the treatment of the King at this time.

"Dr. Monro has lately been frequently in attendance upon the King at Windsor but on these occasions he nor Simmons are not announced to the King, who being blind, is kept in ignorance of their being there. We are spies upon him said Monro for the purpose of judging of his mental and bodily state. Monro was struck with the King's cheerfulness and conversation even in his unhappy state, and said to Hearne:' the King is the pleasantest man I ever came near; of those about him of all degrees he seems to know everything. When not engaged in conversation with them he holds fancied conversations with various characters but mostly with deceased statesmen. His bodily health Monro thinks very good but the malady has much of a fixed character. The reports of Dr. Willis having disapproved of the treatment of His Majesty as prescribed by his Physicians are not true. Dr. Willis has approved of their mode of proceeding.[8]

The following year Farington noted in his diary on 29th May,

'Dr. Monro told me on Wednesday last that he did not think the King would ever recover. He described him to be very cheerful that he passes his time in talking, sometimes to himself and sometimes to those about him, and in playing upon a Harpsichord in an irregular manner. He is, said Dr. Monro, a clever man, has a great deal of knowledge and observation and appears to me to have abilities fully equal to the duties of his station. The general opinion of his capacity is below what he is, which has probably been owing to that hurried manner which has always been manifest in him. In his present unhappy state, he never forgets that he is a

King.' By the end of the year, on the 19th of November, Farington notes: ' Dr. Monro I dined with. Mrs. Monro, J.F. Hearne, Alexander, Dr. Monro (Tom) Miss Monro (Sally), another Miss Monro (possibly Fanny or Julia) and Edridge. Dr. Monro spoke of the King and said that "sometimes he is in a state of great irritation for perhaps 24 hours together but that these attacks had not affected his general health I think." He said "there is a fair probability that the King may live 10 years and were I to lay a wager whether the King or the Prince Regent were to live longer I do not know that I should not bet on the duration of the King's life." It was then remarked that the nervous system of the Prince Regent has been much affected and that he has something about his hands, a twitching which has the appearance of a paralytic affliction....'[14] (The King in fact survived for eight years) By the 3rd September, 1813, Farington noted in his diary that reports had been published in the newspapers that the King was much recovered from his insane state. I spoke to Dr. Monro upon it and was told there was not the least foundation for the reports. He said the King remained as before, going on in a state happy for himself, amusing himself, and often in his conversation very entertaining; that his bodily health was good and that he would probably live longer for being in this state. He spoke further of the effects of insanity and said he did not think that insanity shortens life. I asked him whether in cases where patients appeared to be absorbed in grief it did not cause premature death. He said no, he had not observed that it had that effect. He further said that he did not think that confinement shortens life. He knew cases of very long confinement and the persons continuing in perfect health. Mr. Canning was spoken of and Edridge said he had at one time a great game in his hand and might have risen to the highest situation in the state. He had acted so unsteadily as to lose the confidence of many.'

To return to the year of 1811, when the King was again ill, there is a copy of the questions asked of the physicians, copied by Monro onto the back of an old envelope.

1) Whether from the circumstances detailed in the case, they are able to form any certain or probable opinion of the sphere of the disorder.
2) What general plan of medicine is thought advisable.
3) Whether any particular plan of medicine be thought applicable.
4) Whether any specific medicine can be employed with advantage.
5) Supposing some continued plan of medicine to be recommended is it thought advisable to attempt to force down medicines repeated in the course of the day notwithstanding his aversion and resistance and the consequent irritation to be apprehended.
6) Can any course of management besides what must be obvious to every professional man be suggested.
7) Supposing him more calm and settled wd. it be advisable to represent to him his errors and to check them as they arise or by not noticing them to leave them to subside themselves.

The source of the questions is made clear by a letter from Lambeth Palace:

Dr.Thomas Monro   September 18, 1811

Sir:

I have ye honour to forward to you a case & certain questions founded upon it, as drawn up by ye Physicians in attendance upon His Majesty. You are requested by ye Queen's Council, to consider ye case, and to return written answers to ye questions. You are requested by the same Council to meet Physicians on Sunday next at two o'clock p.m. at Sir Henry Halford's in Curzon Street

I have the honour to be, Sir

Your faithful hle Servant Cantaur

Cantaur wrote again from Lambeth Palace on October 7, 1811, to Dr. Monro at Adelphi Terrace as follows:

"The Queen's Council request yr. attendance of Dr. Monro at Lambeth Palace on Wednesday next in ye morning at twelve o'clock."

Whatever took place at that meeting was not recorded exactly, but a change of heart must have ensued following it, since Cantaur wrote again to Monro:

"Sir: The permission given to you last Saturday to be admitted to His Majesty's apartments separately from Dr. Simmons is suspended. The visits must be made conjointly.

I have Y honour to be Sir
Your faithful hle servant Cantaur

Following this there appeared a letter from the then Prime Minister Spencer Perceval(1809-1812) addressed to Dr. Munro:

"Mr. Perceval Presents his compliments to Doctor Monro and if he could make it convenient to attend at the House of Commons to-morrow at 12 o'clock, His attendance would be very convenient to the proceedings of the Committee appointed this evening for enquiry into the state of His Majesty's Health."

Sp. Perceval Downing Street, Jan. 8th 1812

This was followed by another letter:

"Mr. Perceval presents his compts to Dr. Monro and takes great shame to himself for the mistake in the date of his note. The note was written last night and the Ho.

147

of Co. requesting Dr. Monro's attendance at the House this day."

Downing Street
Jany 10th, 1812

A few other interesting letters have been kept which perhaps should also be quoted since they do enlarge upon the history of the King's illness. Monro seems to have well rewarded for his efforts, at least by the standards of his day.

Sir:

"I am directed by Andw B. Drummond Esqre Keeper of His Majesty's Privy Purse to inform you that he is authorised, and has empowered me, to pay you the sum of £500, for your special attendance on His Majesty, previous to 18th February 1812 on your sending to me your Receipt written on a 5/- stamp, according to the enclosed Form"

I am Sir,
Your most obedient, and most humble servant Hugh Rowland

Privy Purse Office, 7 o'c 17th Sp. 1812

Monro seems to have been prompt in his reply:

"Received of Andw. B. Drummond Esqre. Keeper of His Majesty's Privy Purse Five hundred Pounds for special attendance upon His Majesty previous to the 18th of February, 1812"

Dr. Thomas Monro

Adelphi Terrace

One further letter has been kept:

"Sir:

We have the honour to inform you that his Majesty had rather more than four hours sleep in the night. He has been this morning in good humour, but his conversation has been often incorrect.

We remain Sir, with much respect, Your most obedt. Hubl. servts.

M. Baillie.   David Dundas".[10]

A note in the family records remarks that Thomas Monro prescribed a hop pillow for the King. He may have suggested this as a simple alleviation for sleeplessness, but this also further indicates that he probably had a profound understanding of his patient, if not of the cause of his illness. It was on September 23rd, 1811, that Dr. Baillie came from Windsor to consult the Mad Doctors as they were called, upon the case of the King. Later in November of the same year Farington reported that Dr. Monro was lately in frequent attendance upon the King at Windsor, but on these occasions he and Dr. Simmons are not announced to the King, who being blind was kept in ignorance of their being there. There is one further instance of Monro's treatment of the mentally afflicted which gives another aspect of his character, which was his sense of responsibility, and his refusal to offer suggestions when not in contact with a patient. William Alexander, his great friend who worked at the British Museum, had a mental breakdown in 1816. Mr. Ralph, who appeared to be in charge of him, wrote fully on the treatment he had given him asking for further advice. To William Alexander's brother Monro replied,

"I am truly concerned to hear the accounts you have transmitted to me respecting your brother's malady. As far as I can judge from the account of Mr. Ralph his treatment of the case has been in every way judicious and proper and I should hope by the continuance of his prudent directions your brother will escape any permanent effects of so serious an attack. With respect to giving any directions without personal observation the case I am afraid that will not be advisable as of course the treatment of such disorder must depend upon the nature of its symptoms as they may arise and what may be perfectly proper at one period may be contrary at another. The discretion of the medical attendant, therefore, must be relied on. "[11]

There is nothing recorded in the diary of Tom about visits to Windsor after the year 1812. Once the Prince Regent had been appointed during that time to the Regency, the King seemed left to live in his own world, blind and deaf and left more or less alone, by all the physicians who had originally been called upon to treat him. As he lost all contact with the real world, it has been said that in fact his bodily health improved. His son did little to sway public opinion in favour of the Monarchy, but we are left with none of Monro's opinions, since as we can guess, reading between the lines from the little information that is available, Monro was discreet, even to Farington, and kept most of his opinions to himself. The Prince Regent presented Monro with a gold pencil. Members of the family today are uncertain whether it was for his attendance on the King or for beating the Prince at tennis, a game Monro enjoyed, and played until his legs became "like paste", as he described them to his friend Farington. Meanwhile Monro does not seem to have been consulted about the King on a long term basis, whilst the King himself lived until 1820, blind, deaf and always talking, talking, mostly to himself as he lived on in splendid isolation, losing all contact with reality.

1. Diary of Sir George Baker - Windsor   •
2. Ryl. National Theatre Programme *The Madness of George III* *byM&n* Bennett 1991
3. Private family letters
4. Private letters in possession of Dr. F.G. Jefferiss from Mrs. Dorothy Curtis-Hayward - Monro's grand-daughter.Other original letters are at the
5. Royal College of Physicians (Letters on Monro's visits to Windsor) See also Charles Chenevix Trench *The Royal Malady* Longmans Group U.K. Ltd. 1964
6. Notes are taken from the following: Sir George Baker's Diary and   Sir   Harry Halford's daily record of the illness, Oct. 1811-Jan. 1812 (Windsor) In 1794 Dr.
7. Fordyce made an estimate of symptoms & appearances (after a short summary of his examination the doctor listened to the patients' complaints but royal protocol prevented the dr. from enquiring of the king as to his symptoms). Sir Harry Halford noted in 1795 that the bile duct was excitable.
8. Roy Porter – *History Today* – Vol 36 Issue 11 Nov 1986 p16. See also *A Social History of Madness* Weidenfield & Nicholson, London 1987, also Programme for the Royal National Theatre, play by Alan Bennett *The Madness* of George 111 article by Roy Porter. 1991
9. Jones, K *A history of the Mental Health Services,* 1972 pp75-7
10. *The Diary of Joseph Farington* ed. K. Garlick
11. Ibid
12. All quoted letters in the Collection of Royal College of Physicians. Envelope in a private collection of the family.
13. Family collection (photocopy with author)

CHAPTER 7 – BETHLEM HOSPITAL

Towards the end of his time as superintendent at Bethlem, frequently referred to as Bedlam, Thomas Monro had to undergo an enquiry into the running of the Hospital. Since this was to prove a major event in the life of the doctor it is necessary to go into detail on the case, which brought him before the House of Commons to answer questions that had been raised in the public press. By studying in detail the conditions under which those considered insane were kept at the beginning of the nineteenth-century, and how Monro answered to the charges brought against him, a great deal is revealed about the man himself, as well as the state of the poor unfortunates who came under his care. It was a moment when Monro had to answer for his chosen career as a physician of madness, in a business he had inherited, not by inclination but by obligation, as being a family concern, following the death of his brother John. He was charged with neglecting his patients. The enquiry took place in early May in the year 1816.

Bethlem Hospital had not enjoyed a very good reputation during the previous century, since James Monro (1728-1772) had accompanied the artist Hogarth "with casebook and a running commentary."[1]   The pictures that resulted have become fact by legend, being well known works, rather than by an understanding as to how Hogarth may have exaggerated what he saw in order to sell a more imaginative scene.   During his tenure James Monro refused to admit students or physicians before 1743 to see his work, which apparently was one of the reasons why St. Luke's hospital was founded, 'so that more gentlemen of the faculty could study the branch of physic too long confined almost to a single person.'   It would seem that James Monro did not seek to keep his manner of practise a secret, but recorded how he thought it 'disingenious to perplex mankind with points that must for ever remain intricate and uncertain.' Under his son John Monro, Thomas's father, physician to the Hospital from 1752-1792, changes began to take place. By 1769 a Resident Medical Officer had been appointed, referred to as an Apothecary. John Monro tried to give the patients more tranquility, privacy and medical attention. The holiday crowds were abolished, since before the lunatics had been on public view. Measures were taken to keep the neighbourhood of the bedrooms free from a noisy watchhouse, and the keepers were instructed to examine the feet of patients every night and morning, who were lying on straw or in chairs. In such cases the feet were apt to mortify (as Thomas Monro was later to report) unless regularly chafed or covered with flannel. By 1780, on John Monro's advice, vegetables and better beer were allowed, which eliminated the scurvy. Officials at the Hospital became better paid, to encourage them to forego 'perks'. In 1788 the superiority of Bedlam over the French hospitals is described by a Frenchman, with Bethlem described as clean and cheerful.[2] John Monro bundled all cases of hallucination and religious melancholia into the hospital without argument, and the apothecary was ordered to apply a blister to each, in contrast to John Wesley's spiritual remedies. He was described by Wesley's Mother as "that wretched fellow Monro", but John Monro seems genuinely to have attempted to improve the lot of his patients within the understanding of his time. Another of his changes was that admission was by ticket only, as a member of the public, which suggests that those who were admitted were strictly controlled. We know that Dr. John also attempted to stop the feasting with which the governors indulged themselves each year at the expense of the charities.

John Monro was perhaps best known for his *Treatise on Madness,* which he wrote in defence of Dr. Battie's remarks. John Monro wrote that "Madness is a distemper of such a nature that very little of real use can be said concerning it. The immediate causes will forever disappoint our search and the cure of that disorder depends on management as much as medicine." (These last words were quoted by Thomas in his defence.) John Monro goes on to say that he is writing in answer to the "undeserved censures which Dr. Battie has thrown on my predecessors." The censure seems to refer to Battie's remarks that the defect in knowledge at that time on 'lunatics' was that their care had been entrusted to ' empiricks ', or at best to a few select physicians, most of whom thought it advisable to keep the cases as well as the patients to themselves. When Pitt defeated C.J. Fox in 1784, there was a well known caricature of Doctor John with Fox in a strait jacket with straws in his hair, represented as having gone raving mad in consequence of this catastrophe. Doctor John, as the physician of Bethlem, is depicted as having ordered the removal of Fox to the incurable ward. This was only an event in the artist's imagination, but obviously thought to be a dreadful fate.

Dr. Thomas must have been well thought of as a Physician by his contemporaries, as he was made censor of the Royal College of Physicians in 1792, 1799 and 1812, also Harveian Orator in 1799, and named an Elect in 1811, as well as being Principal Physician to Bethlem and Bridewell Hospitals from 1792 to 1816. He had a large private practice including such members of the aristocracy as Lord Lyttleton, the Duchess of Norfolk and the Duchess of Chandos, also a private lunatic asylum, Brook House in Hackney. There is no doubt that the hospital, nicknamed Bedlam, was in an unsatisfactory state at that time, and must have been difficult to manage in its last days in Moorfields, before moving to the new premises at Lambeth. Monro seems to have been a man of great energy who filled his day with medical work and his evenings with his interest in the arts, not only in drawing and painting but the theatre as well. There is no evidence that he neglected his work for the sake of art, but it is evident from the trouble at Bethlem, alluded to in his son's diaries, that perhaps he lacked administrative and practical ability. He was not re-appointed as Physician to Bethlem in 1816, because it seems that he had not supervised the management of the hospital properly, but had occupied himself with clinical work. He had left the routine administration of the hospital to the resident apothecary, with a steward who was incapable through age and drunkenness. Thomas Monro had to undergo an enquiry into the running of Bethlem Hospital in 1816. Unfortunately the diaries of Edward Thomas, his son, are missing for both that and the following year. It was a long defence, and the length of the 'Observations' as well as the verbosity of the language seem to make it desirable to give a summary where possible of the details, although preserving Thomas Monro's own words as much as possible. He had to answer both to a Committee of Enquiry before the House of Commons, and to the Governors of Bedlam. His answers to the Governors cover most of the questions that had been raised by the Committee of Enquiry. Monro began his defence as follows:

"I find myself, after having for more than thirty years filled the office of physician without the slightest imputation on my conduct, suddenly charged with undefined offences, and exposed, without the consciousness of guilt, to the painful humiliation of an abrupt suspension. I am called up to offer reasons in my justification, without precisely knowing against what charges I am to justify myself, and am compelled to frame my own accusation in order to enter upon my defence."[3]

Farington also reported in his diary on 6th May, 1816,"Edridge called in the evening. He spoke of Dr. Monro being in a very unpleasant situation in consequence of a Committee having been appointed to examine into the state of Bedlam Hospital for lunatics. Dr. Monro succeeded his father as first physician to this hospital which appears, upon investigation, to have for sometime been much neglected by the officers who have the care of it and great abuses have been committed. Dr. Monro is inculpated in these charges so far as to have been neglectful in not seeing properly to the state of the Hospital. Edward Wakefield has been the active agent of the Committee and continues to be so. He has very much urged Dr. Monro to 'resign his situation which would be prejudiced to his reputation as a physician and probably to him in other respects; that he is in great trouble and anxiety to prevent this evil.' Edridge has been (in touch) with the Rt. Hon. Chas Long on the subject who will do what he can to enable Dr. Monro to continue in the institution."[4]

DMonro may have filled his evenings with social interests, and his interest in the arts, not only in drawings but in his concerns with young artists, and also in the theatre. However, there is no evidence of his neglect of his duties. Farington in 1796 reported that: "He (Monro) told us that his professional situation does not allow of his quitting London for several days together. He has not been four days together absent from London in four years". From 1806, his son Tom repeatedly mentions in his diary his father's frequent visits to hospitals, and patients, and how even when he was staying at his house at Bushey, he travelled almost daily to London. He was consulted on at least ten occasions at Windsor, although no written record remains of his thoughts when he was consulted about the King. Medical knowledge was limited, and taking as an example the treatment of his son Henry in his last illness, who was under the care of one of the foremost physicians of his day, yet the best this physician could do was to bleed him with leeches, blister him to such an extent that his family and friends had to treat the burns, and give him a clyster. Henry was complaining of a cough. So it was with the treatment of the insane, and although the conditions under which they were kept had improved, there was little advance in knowledge as to how to actually treat many of the patients.[5]

A letter had been published in the daily papers in May, 1816, and circulated amongst the Governors, which contained specific charges against Thomas Monro. It was inferred that Monro had been deficient in his duty, and this was one of the charges that he had to defend himself against. The charges were listed, and the first was that he had been wanting in humanity towards the unhappy objects who were placed under his care as patients in the Hospital. The second was that Monro had pursued a course of medical treatment indiscriminate in its applications, cruel in itself, useless in his own opinion and injurious in that of others. The third point was that Monro had been guilty of neglect in his attendance at the Hospital, and in the performance of his duties in his office of physician. Monro had been physician at the Hospital since 1783, and the gentleman who was the resident physician, referred to as the Apothecary, was a Mr. Haslam. The first charge mentioned several patients by name. The answers he gave are summarised.

c   "I would not have it supposed that I wish to shield myself behind this report if it should be the pleasure of the Court to direct it and I prepared to defend myself. In the case of James Tilley Matthews levelled against the Governors as well as myself and the visiting members of the College of Physicians for detaining as a lunatic someone not a proper object for restraint, I merely refer to the judgement of the visiting members of the College of Physicians as supporting my own. As to the case of Miss Stone, the crowded state of the Hospital made classification impossible. She was in the habit of tearing her clothing, and continued to the last hour completely insensible to the calls of nature, although the extreme kindness of the present matron had induced her to bestow on this unfortunate lady particular attention. I entirely dismiss the charge of inhumanity. The imposing of restraint upon the patients makes no part of the duty of physician, but is expressly confided to the Apothecary. It is not imposed for strictly medical reasons, but to prevent mischief. Such restraint as has been found necessary has been specially applied to incurable patients: none have been received as incurable but such as have exhibited proof of being dangerous to themselves or others are restrained. If the physician, whose visits are only occasional, interfered in matters of this kind he might, in desiring to promote the comfort of the patients be really exposing the staff as well as the patients themselves to danger. The Governors have thought fit to repose such confidence in the Apothecary that 'no patient is to be confined in chains, nor released from such confinement without his consent."

In addition he added"The medical treatment of the patients, as to which there has been so unfortunate (a) misconstruction. . . of my evidence before the Committee of the House of Commons, that I must intrude upon the Governors in detail." Now followed the summary of a curious custom, explained by Monro.

r   "In the summer months, medicine is generally administered, and not in the winter, the cold rendering it improper - general remedies, bleeding, purging and vomiting are not applied to those unfit for it. . . that such remedies are 'Exhibited' on particular days and only to those patients who require them. The Physician generally communicates with the Apothecary, but much is left to his discretion. He used frequently to go round the house with the Apothecary and point out to him which he thought the proper patients to undergo the necessary operations. Those patients to whom the course of medicine was not expected to be useful were exempted from it. Bleeding did not take place indiscriminately without reference to the habits of the patient, though sometimes he (the physician) left it to the Apothecary (to decide on treatment). If a difference of opinion existed between myself and the Apothecary as to vomiting, as to which I followed, as I was bound to do, my own judgement. The patients were ordered to be bled either the beginning or end of May according to the weather and the season late or early, followed by a certain number of vomits and then purged. This course of treatment had been practised by my father and was in my own opinion beneficial. Medicine was administered when necessary at other periods and the medical operations adopted in the Hospital are similar to those pursued in my own house (his private medical home Brook House) The insane are cured more by management than by medicine, but it is necessary to give medicine at particular times."

Monro then mentioned the letter of complaint, and the Governors' question as to whether this treatment was cruel when he, the physician informed them that it was useless. He answered.

"I would ask any gentleman to point out a single passage which intimates my opinion that it (medicine) is useless: and I would venture to rest the whole decision upon what must be the reply to this question. Have I not in the same sentence, almost in the same breath said that it was necessary at particular times? And could any one have been induced for a moment to suppose that I said it was useless, unless a part of my evidence had been separated and brought forward for the purpose. Medicine is not the only nor even the principal cure, in most cases it may be useful and in some necessary. Seclusion, diet and moral management, as it has been

159

termed, are of the first and most essential importance. If I expressed reluctance to make this opinion public, it proceeded from a consciousness that it militated against the prejudices of the world at large that ascribes much greater efficacy to the powers of medicine in cases of insanity than it can be fairly said to possess. I inherit the opinion, in some measure, from one whose judgement had been formed by long experience and whose skill, deservedly stood high in the estimation of his contemporaries, notwithstanding the reflection attempted to be cast upon it in the Letter so often alluded to. It agrees too with many who now adorn the profession in this country and a very eminent French physician. I would not have it supposed that I neglect the use of medicine as I have expressly stated to the Committee of the House of Commons. Whenever patients require medicine for their mental disease they have it." The supposition that a patient received in October would stand no chance of being cured by any application of science until the following spring was wholly unfounded. Journals now kept of the medical proceedings in the New Hospital could fully testify to this.

Monro, it is recorded, continued in his defence:

"With respect to the merits of the mode of treatment which I have practised consisting chiefly of evacuents as a general rule I know no better. From long experience in the peculiar malady I feel entitled to rest on my private judgement. Numerous opinions concur in representing these to be the principle remedies, and indeed the very frequent termination of the disease in palsy or apoplexy, affords a strong indication of the course to be pursued. Various other modes of treatment have been occasionally adopted, the results of which being far from satisfactory, have served only to confirm me in my adherence to my usual practice. The supposition of the cruelty of this practice can only be founded on that of its inutility, and the idea that I myself believed it to be useless is so extravagant in itself that had it not been publicly proclaimed I confess I should have doubted the possibility of its being entertained by any sober or rational mind."

Monro mentions his long professional experience and his feelings that the system he had pursued was the most likely to be productive. He also answered to the accusation that he only applied medicine at certain stated periods of the year without discrimination, and without regard to the particular cases of individuals. He certainly seems to have held interesting opinions as to what took place regarding his patients during the Spring.

"The great alteration which takes place in the spring of the year is not confined to vegetable nature but the animal world experiences it; a more active circulation takes place throughout the human body, inflammatory diseases of all description begin to show themselves and a counteracting system of medical treatment has to be adopted. The character of lunacy often assumes a different aspect at this season and some patients, even incurable lunatics, exhibit a more violent display of their insanity at the approach of summer, whilst some get greater relief from medicine and are restored to sanity."
He reported that the extreme coldness of the late Hospital (Moorfields) resulted in mortification of the feet, which as maniacs they were more liable to than other persons, "it being found, by experience, that the extremities of patients are peculiarly subject to chilliness, resulting from a determination of blood towards the head. If the treatment were used in the winter, the tendency to mortification would be greater from the debility it is likely to produce. Lunatics, in a

cold Hospital like Bethlem could not bear evacuations in the cold weather as "they are in the habit of frequently pulling off their clothes; will throw the straw out of their cribs, and are sometimes found in the morning stark naked upon the floor." In the short days they were locked up in their cells for 14 or 15 hours, and it was not surprising that those whose "reasoning faculties are almost obliterated suffer from the severity of the cold." Summarising his report, Monro added that the perspiration which followed vomiting would be checked in the cold weather; the sudden and opposite changes in the circulation would be counteracted by the application of cold air to the surface of the skin and expose the patient to various bodily diseases. In the shortness of a winter day to give vomits would interfere with the patient's meals. Cathartic medicines are given during this season when necessary and when particular indications present themselves, but to pursue a regular course in winter would be impracticable. If confined to their cells the patients would be subjected to the cold occasioned by the wet straw and to consequent diseases. In summer the operation of medicine is over before they retire to rest and the straw changed before they are shut up for the night. The small staff could not pay enough attention to patients undergoing a course of medicine in winter.Out of the whole number of curable patients in Bethlem Hospital there were few to whom the present system might not be applied with advantage, and therefore generally, though not indiscriminately applied. In many instances the selection was confined to the Apothecary. The fairest test was in practical results. Monro then stated: "The proportion of patients cured in Bethlem will bear comparison with any other public institution of a similar description. Of 293 patients admitted during three years ending 1st January, 1816, the number discharged was 119. St. Luke's admissions in three years ending 1st January, 1814, there was 870 patients, with 358 reported cures, as near as possible two fifths of the gross number of admissions in both hospitals. This exceeds somewhat that of the Hospital Charenton in France, which estimated one third. At Bethlem the proportion of admissions subsequent to the exposition of the management of the hospital before the Committee of the House of Commons has not been lessened, which must have been the inevitable consequence of the truth of the proposition. The numbers at St. Luke's are extremely low. It can accommodate 300 patients and on 29th February last, there were 264. No public notice had yet been given that the New Hospital is open for the reception of patients, though it had been generally known that the old one had been pulled down. No incurables are now admitted into Bethlem, and the War being now ended the number of patients being sent from Transport and War Offices is materially decreased. Also various establishments for the cure of insanity have been recently erected in different parts of the country under the provision of a late Act of Parliament. The falling off in numbers is stated in the Evidence to be common to Bethlem and St. Lukes."

In answer to the charge of neglect in attendance at the Hospital and in the performance of the duties of his office, Monro gave further details.

"The duties of the Physician", he stated, "is to attend the resident officers, servants and others employed at either Hospital (St. Luke's) when ill. He also should have to inform the Committee of any neglect or abuse and suggest such reforms as he may think necessary. He has to attend every meeting of the Sub-Committee at Bethlem, to take in and discharge patients, and on every Monday and Wednesday he has to attend at the said

Hospital to examine and prescribe for the patients, the Monday during the bathing season excepted. Excepting when ill, or prevented by some very particular circumstances, uniformly I have attended after the Hospital as often as required of me, witness the Apothecary and Keepers," Monro stated. "The Steward gave evidence before the House of Commons 'that he believed I attended but seldom'. He has since corrected this statement. As the steward had only been lately appointed he was not aware that it was customary for those patients who were ill to be seen by the Physician in his private room in the Hospital and his not seeing him in the Galleries very often led him to suppose the visits were infrequent."

Monro added that from subsequent information the steward, on finding that he attended two or three times a week according to the season, except when his son attended to prescribe for or admit patients, had retracted his statement. Monro admitted not having gone around the galleries to examine every patient, because he considered it would be useless and impracticable, unless sufficient time were allowed for the consideration of every case, and the incessant clamour and confusion prevailing in the galleries would impede the physician if not entirely prevent the performance of his duty. Only three minutes could be allowed for the examination of each case as there were sometimes nearly 300 and rarely less than 120. It seemed that more could be done by examining with care into those cases brought forward by the Apothecary, who saw every case every day, rather than for the physician to see every case twice a week, and he is nowhere directed to do so. Monro added that there was an examination in a private room of all new patients admitted since the preceding visiting day, both as to mental malady and bodily health, and this determined the mode of treatment by the indications which presented themselves. In addition he added that he occasionally walked into some of the Galleries (wards) to view them. He felt such perambulations were injurious to many patients as the very appearance of the physician "creates excitement in their minds not easily allayed, and they "sometimes have to be confined to their cells till they become more calm and tractable."

Monro continued his evidence on the charges that the Physician did not visit any case not specially reported. This charge had been given by the Matron, who was not aware that patients were sent for to Monro's private room, when he paid his visits to the Hospital two or three times a week, since she had only been a short time in the situation of Matron. Her statement to the House of Commons had since been corrected by letter to the Chairman of the Committee. Another charge that the bodily complaints of patients were unattended to was utterly refuted. Monro told the Board of Governors, under the chairmanship of the Rt. Hon. George Rose, that it was expressly stated by one of the keepers (Simmonds) in his examination before the House of Commons that they were attended to at all times. (Evidence, 1815 - p.74 Regulations, p.59) The last charge against abuses to which it had been insinuated that Dr. Monro was privy were the drunkenness of the keepers and the imbecility of the steward. Monro replied that the servants' intoxication had already been mentioned before the House of Commons in the case of the then porter, as having been reported to the steward and members of the Sub-Committee. The supervision of servants was the immediate duty of the steward. Complaints should be made to the Sub-Committee by him and not to the physician, who had mentioned these cases to several members of the Sub-Committee. However, there did seem to be a problem here, because Monro further elaborated that the steward's imbecility was due to age. The Sub-Committee was aware of his state as they transacted business with him weekly, and he did not feel it was his responsibility to point out the growing infirmities of an old servant. Monro may not have known about these two individuals, and it did seem as if any responsibility that they may have held was not in competent hands. It should perhaps be the responsibility of someone in charge to have been aware of the situation and to have dealt with it, or at least to have used more force in persuading the Sub-Committee that all was not well and that this was a situation that had to be dealt with.

Apparently evidence given before the Committee of the House of Commons stated that the late surgeon of the hospital was incapacitated by drunkenness or insanity. Monro reported that he saw him very seldom. The surgeon only attended on particular cases of patients -"those who had met with accidents or had disorders that required his assistance." These were very few and there was scarcely any communication with reference to our professional duties. They met usually when the Physician attended Sub-Committees. If anything had there manifested itself in his behaviour obvious to the members of the Sub-Committee, it would have been as evident to them as to Monro. Monro stated he had no reason to believe that he was either drunken or insane.

The Rt. Hon George Rose, in the chair at the Board of Governor's enquiry, questioned Monro closely, and this showed up one or two points of detail, namely that Monro and the Apothecary Haslam were not always in agreement. Apparently Mr. Haslam expressed in his book that in his opinion vomiting was generally unfavourable. To this Monro replied "I vomit my patients freely." Afterwards he purged them. Monro's comment was "that has been the practice invariably for years, long before my time - it was handed down to me by my father -I do not know any better practice." If a patient was to become extremely violent and furious, he would be purged and bled. George Rose then asked Monro: "Would you treat a private individual patient at your own house in the same way as has been described in respect of Bethlem?"

"Certainly not", replied Monro, and went on to explain that neither in physicking or bleeding would they receive the same treatment. There were no chains in a private house, and no occasion for such a number of servants.

"Are you of the opinion that as much care is taken in the medical treatment of each individual in Bethlem as is done in your own private house?"

"I should suppose so. Very little depends upon me because I am very seldom there, comparatively speaking with the apothecary - he is there every day - a vast deal of the medical treatment must depend upon him. "

Rose continued" What are your objections to chains and fetters as a mode of restraint?"

"I never gave orders for a patient to be put in irons in the whole course of my life. They are fit only for pauper lunatics. If a gentleman was put into irons, he would not like it. Pauper lunatics, of course, cannot pay for the regular attendance to prevent them doing mischief, and there are so few servants kept for the purpose - that it is the only mode of restraining them." However, Monro continued, that in order to prevent them from doing mischief both to themselves or any other person, he recommended a waistcoat. "I consider a strait waistcoat a much better thing than irons." The waistcoat would be kept on only" when it was immediately necessary, and would at the first opportunity be taken off and eased. There was no idea of preventing respiration."

"Do you think a man in superior rank of life is more likely in a state of insanity to be irritated by irons than a pauper lunatic?"

"Most assuredly. It may retard recovery. Irons," Monro continued, "were used for a most ferocious and mischievous madman, who said he would do for somebody."

"Do you think it is within the scope of medical knowledge to discover any other efficacious means of treating insane persons with respect to the means used?"

"I really do not depend a vast deal upon medicine", Monro replied. "I do not think medicine is the sheet anchor. It is more by management that those persons are cured than by medicine, but it is necessary to give medicine at particular times. The disease is not cured by medicine in my opinion. If I am obliged to make that public, I must do so."[6]

On 16th May, Farington reported in his diary that he say The Times of today, in which was published that 'yesterday at a meeting at Bridewell Dr. Monro and Mr. Haslam, the two medical attendants at Bethlem Hospital were removed from their situation. The votes were for Dr. Monro, for his removal 45, against 35, whilst Mr. Haslam had only 4 for his being continued.'[7]   Edward Thomas took over his father's duties at Bethlem.

It has not been exactly recorded how the welfare of the patients at Bedlam changed once Edward Thomas was in charge, but it certainly changed. An interesting description has come down from the diary of Lady Eastlake, written in 1844, when on March 24th she visited Bedlam:

"Drove to Bedlam, a former Palace of Henry Vlll. Lord Shaftesbury, Mr. Dewar and two other Governors joined us. Lord S. knowing all the patients, as we went through two female wards. Altogether the sense of the pervading humanity and benevolence, and judgement of the institution far overpowered all sense of pain at its purpose and need. It was refreshing to catch a sane eye among the many wild, moody, cunning, silly or vacant, even a sane cat stretched on a sill in the sun was delightful. Above 50 patients in the State-Patients ward. I was much struck by the division of the classes. Eight women sat in (a) small, light room, carpeted and curtained with bookcases, piano and round table."[8]

There is little doubt that the events of the year of 1816, when Thomas Monro was removed from his position at Bethlem Hospital changed him a great deal. Following this his good friend William Alexander had died in July of that year, and not long after this his friend Hearne. In the family there is a letter from his brother Charles, dated March 11th, 1802, from 'Ashted', in which Charles casts grave doubts on the way the Bethlem Hospital was being run. He was looking at it from the point of view of the accounts, and realised that Monro's remuneration was going to be very small indeed, and he was requesting at this time, permission to carry out a thorough investigation. Charles Monro continued in his letter:

"Apropros of Haslam -1 think he is in danger of getting into a Scrape - He has stated the Sum necessary to be allowed him as an equivalent for what he has been in the habit of receiving in kind from the Hospital at £350 per annum - when to that is added his Salary of £100 and gratuity of £50 - his place will appear to be worth to him £500 per year beside House, Rent and Fares, which cannot be estimated at less than £60 a year more. All this entre nous."

It would appear that long before the House of Commons Hearing Monro had plenty to worry about, so it is small wonder that his own health began to deteriorate. There is no evidence that Monro neglected his work for the sake of art, but it is evident from the trouble at Bethlem, that the hospital was in an unsatisfactory state. It may have been difficult to manage in its last days in Moorfields in 1814-15, waiting to move into its new premises, but the treatment used there was certainly the standard method of the time. It does seem from both his son's diaries, and subsequent events, that Monro lacked administrative and practical ability. His portraits, made by his son Henry before 1813 showed the doctor as plump and healthy, but the last two that Henry drew before he died, already showed his father having undergone a rapid change, making him appear an older and thinner man. Not only did his abscess, and his stomach complaint take their toll, but it would seem that financial worries might also have been a debilitating factor.

1. O'Donaghue, E.G. The Story of Bethlehem Hospital 1914 London
2. Ibid
3. Extract from the Thomas Enquiry before the Governors of the Hospital - taken from the Committee of Enquiry report held by the College of Physicians, London.
4. Cave, Kathryn ed. Diaries of Joseph Farington 1816 Vol.   p.
5. Jefferiss - F.G. See his Biography of Thomas Monro for the 1976 V&A Catalogue
6. See report held by the College of Physicians
7. Cave, Kathryn ed. Diaries of Joseph Farington 1816
8. Journals and Correspondence of Lady Eastlake Vol. 1

CHAPTER 8 – WATERCOLOURS AND RETIREMENT

Already before the death of Henry, Monro's health was failing, and he began to give up more and more of his duties and responsibilities to his eldest son Tom, who was by this time married, settled in Gower Street and quite competent to take on a large share of his father's work. In April of 1817, almost a year after the Government Enquiry, Dr. Thomas handed over to his son a quarter from his share in the profits of Brook House, and one third of his fees, and Tom records many hours spent over the Brook House accounts. We seem to have further proof here that the senior doctor did not have much inclination to keep these in good order. As in the case at Bethlem, the financial aspects of his business were not of major concern to Monro. Tom was also working at this time at the Brompton Hospital for the Cox family, for which his father-in-law paid him thirty seven pounds, ten shillings per quarter. Dr. Heberden was the chief physician at this time at Brompton.

By 1818 Tom's financial position was becoming assured, for he tells of paying £300 to Mr. Cox, his father-in-law, probably cancelling a loan. It was just as well that he should be independent and begin to be personally successful, in addition to helping his father, for all through that year the health of his father was not good. Just after his fifty ninth birthday, (29th May) Tom recorded "My father ill at Bushey." Periods of ill health seemed to increase throughout his old age. There is seldom any mention in Tom's diary of the artistic side of his father's life, other than annual visits to the Royal Academy and the British Institute openings. With a wife and growing family of his own, as well as a busy life which included Brompton, as well as his duties at the Foundling Hospital, Bethlem, Brook House and Bridewell, it is surprising that he did manage to keep a watchful eye on his father, and keep up his diary. He wrote again in his diary for 18th August, "to Town early and found my father much unwell in the Adelphi"

It is surprising that Tom does not also make a note of what his problems were, since being a doctor himself, this should have been of interest, but the diary seldom had any medical notes and seemed to be kept for family events of interest.

The following year Tom was 'in consultation' with the family concerning the future of the little boys, as he often referred to his younger brothers in his diary. Robert was at Oxford, where he took his B.A. on 18th May, 1819, but the younger ones were about to be taken from Harrow, and their future was of family importance. Uncle Charles, the lawyer, was present at this meeting, along with Doctors Powell and Roberts, following this they dined together, when Edridge also joined them, as did Tom. Little more is recorded by Tom concerning this event, but he did record that Jack had received his medal 'at the Arts and Sciences', presumably just before he left Harrow. Monro himself was again unwell, and had another attack of dysentery, but seemed to have recovered in time to start on his planned tour to the Wye, initially with Sally, Jack and Alex, but with no mention of Hannah Monro. They stayed at Ross-on-Wye, at the Duchess of Norfolk's Holme Lacy, although Tom gives us little about the details as to why this lodging was chosen. Bob joined them by the 8th July. Four days later Tom records, 'My father and party crossed the Severn at Chepstow and went to Bath.' This would have been by ferry. From there they visited many places, including Somerton, Stourhead, Stonehenge and Overton. Bob left the party at Bath, and travelled to London, and then to Brighton, having 'collected his passport from the French Ambassador'. He met up with his friend James Earle, and they seem to have taken a comprehensive tour of Switzerland, and France, obviously carefully planned by Tom, since he seemed to be able to record exactly where they were travelling.   Shortly after the return of Monro and his children to Bushey, Alex left and having collected his passport, travelled to Calais, and then to Boulogne, where he met up with Edridge.   There are few details remaining, other than a letter from Edridge to his friend Monro, which confirms that he was in France, and that he had seen both boys in Boulogne, which presumably included Bob on his return trip from Switzerland. Monro had taken Jack, the youngest, and gone on a tour of Sussex, to see friends. Robert meanwhile returned to Oxford to take his Master's Degree, which he did on 15th November, 1821, and sometime during this period, or before the end of the year, he also married his cousin Charlotte Monro, daughter of his Uncle James from Hadley.   He was ordained by the Bishop of Gloucester at St. Martin in the Fields in 1822.

Edridge wrote several letters to Monro from France, keeping in close touch, at a time when Monro and his family were on their travels to the Wye. Since he was already travelling there, was no doubt why Tom had asked him to be of use in meeting the Monro boys, which he does not mention in June, so they may have travelled a little later.

Paris, June 17th, 1819

Edridge writes that his friends have now left him and he has a moment to write.

"Sir George (Beaumont) is, as you know, a delightful companion, but there is a perpetual fidget about him, that is tiresome to the greatest degree, and then he is all doctrine and no practice, very little has been done in the way of sketching and by him not a touch. They quitted Paris yesterday for Switzerland and I am left to my own course. It is a most amusing place and I wish you were here with me."- - -"If you have a mind for a trip, now is your time. There are coaches and cabriolets at Rouen (where Edridge went after Paris) in abundance. I was sketching Notre Dame today, and I met an English artist – Mr. Nash, who draws Gothic architecture."[1]

From the letter it is possible that Edridge realised, that without mentioning the availability of coaches, the doctor would not travel, as by this time he was beginning to become quite lame, making moving about a difficulty. Meanwhile perhaps Mr. Nash, the well known architect of Regent Street and Portland Place in London, amongst other areas, was gaining further inspiration from a study of Notre Dame. There is a letter on the family files, written by Edridge on 20th July, 1818, who had been touring the west country, Bath and Taunton, with his young son who was very unwell with consumption. His son died the day he wrote to his great friend Monro, to pour out his misery, at a time when he seems to have lost two other old friends, followed by his son. His trip to France seems to have been his first journey since that sad time the year before.

In 1820, when Monro was aged sixty one, Monro told Farington that he proposed to retire to Bushey, where he would furnish a room with drawings, as that would now be his family residence. He bought five Canaletto drawings from Farington to make a start. He considered that he himself had arrived at the time of life when it became fit for him to devote his mind to serious reflection. Much against his wife's wishes they left Adelphi Terrace that year, and moved permanently to Bushey. From here he carried on his practice which gradually became smaller until about five years later he had ceased to visit any patients. He occupied himself while at home with working on his collection of drawings in the octagonal room in the middle of the house, lit by a sky light, usually dressed in a loose wrapper or dressing gown, and visited by his children and grandchildren in total patriarchal style. He pasted drawings all over the walls of his room, nailing strips of wood between them to give the appearance of frames, as he had previously done at Adelphi Terrace. In the snowy weather he would have the garden paths swept and artificial blooms put in the flower beds as he disliked the lack of colour. He often visited his son Tom at home, first at Gower Street and later at Bedford Place, to view a current exhibition, sometimes staying the night to attend a dinner at the Thatched House Club, but otherwise returning home the same day. He had many friends in and around Bushey, including Lord Essex at Cassiobury Park, whom he seems to have visited frequently. As he found difficulty in walking he rode everywhere, even in the church yard. Farington reported in 1817 that "Monro gave a poor account of his own health, said he could not walk 300 yards, but could ride 20 miles. Had not drunk any wine for the last two years and sleeps better, - good opinion of the blue pill, a preparation of Calomel, which he takes occasionally." He also reports Thomas Hearne as saying that "he (Hearne) gave an indifferent account of Dr. Monro who calls upon him almost every second day. He says the doctor complains of much disorder in his stomach with excessive heart burn" In spite of all this he survived to the age of seventy three and seems to have led an active life almost to the end. Many of his artist friends visited him at home, perhaps talking about the change in style that had evolved in the acceptance of water colours. Perhaps it may be of interest to describe the changes in style since Monro had first begun his evening meetings.

There is no certain evidence that the doctor ever used water colour, although there are several colour-washed drawings attributed to him. He did not sign or date any of his drawings, or entitle them. According to family tradition he used to refer to his drawings as his 'imaginings'. In almost every specimen of his work there is the Indian Ink outline to be found, sometimes very slight but sufficient to form a guide to the main idea. Taking one drawing as an example a very few lines are visible, just outlining the banks of a stream. The rest of the picture is entirely in monochrome wash. The slow current is emphasised by the reflections. The irregularities of the foreground banks are shown by the varied strength of tone. The sky, the distance and the flat stretch of fields are all depicted in the simples washes, the whole effect being one of great beauty and space. It seems very probable that the few outlines were Dr. Thomas' memory of some stream or trees he had noticed as he rode about the country, and the rest was the outcome of his imagination, or perhaps an impression which the style of another artist's work had made on him.

Only in retirement did the doctor finally have time to visit that popular tourist area of the early 1800's, the Wye valley, which was an area which the Rev. William Gilpin had written much about in his guide book, and advocated this as an area which should be visited by the picturesque tourist. Gilpin's lessons on massing, the importance of light and shade, and irregular forms, were important lessons that were absorbed by the emerging group of young professional artists, although the instructions had been written for the gentle amateur, who were increasing in number, as they travelled taking their sketchbooks with them. At a time when Monro had so many young artists meeting in his house, where they had every opportunity to take an interest in his many books, discussions must have come up on contemporary literature. It was in opposition to Gilpin's ideas that notable artists had to learn to create exciting effects in their watercolours, not easily attained by the mere amateur. It was also at this time that poetry and literature were very influential for many travellers, who wanted to see areas that had been written about. Gilpin gave the impression that by using his model of sketching with a Claude glass, an oval box with a blackened mirror, which was slightly convex, a "claudian" view of a scene was reduced to a size suitable for a sketch block or canvas.

The glass could be held in the hand, and the use of a blackened rather than an ordinary mirror gave a somewhat weak reflection, so as to stress the 'framed' and prominent views in the landscape, picking out the high points of foreground and middle ground, whilst the background, Gilpin advocated, should be brightly lit. At the expense of details the Claude glass lowered the colours. Monro would not have approved of such an idea, but he certainly had the urge to go and see the country around the Wye valley for himself.

Pictures were works in the medium of oil paint. A drawing was made in Tiental ink, or with pen, charcoal, lead pencil or brush alone, and this afterwards was 'stained', using a wash of water colour. In the late eighteenth century, grey was felt to be the union of all primary colours, whilst broken colours were those which were mixed with faint white. Opaque colour, or colour mixed with white, was used by many artists, because when added to pigments, this could create a much softer tone, but white also became unnecessary as gradually it was realised that the pure white surface of paper, either by itself or in small well-defined portions could be used by moistening the colour with a 'hair pencil', or removing the colour entirely with an absorbent rag (or balls of bread in Turner's case), so as to render more transparent the colour that remained. The main step in advance of the theory was the direct use of local colour, which raised the work from being a mere drawing to the dignity of a painting. It is a mystery why it should have taken so long a succession of artists to prepare the way. The explanation seems to lie in motive for action , with a gradual advance in technique, which culminated in the days of Turner's maturity. Paul and Thomas Sandby's tinted drawings, outlined with a pen, shaded in grey and finished with washes of local colour, were mostly drawn on common writing paper. The four greatest practitioners, J.R.Cozens, Thomas Girtin, J.M.W. Turner and John Sell

Cotman, all used procedures which varied from the usual method. They used the white paper for the highest lights and built up transparent washes one over another, to obtain gradations of colour and of tone. However once exposed to the ideas of Monro, Hearne and Edridge, they began to experiment with coloured papers as well, especially Girtin, who used brown paper. Monro himself preferred light blue paper, although recorded in the diary of his son, was a note that he sent to Paris for paper with a peach bloom to it.

Many Monro drawings in charcoal or India ink, have been preserved and can be seen in many collections, some represented by the various illustrations here. These drawings show a depth of feeling, a sense of composition, and a truth of tone, which leave no doubt as to his gifts as an artist. The sketches were made out of doors on a 'pad' (or block in modern terminology), in Payne's grey or Indian-ink wash, sometimes on grey, sometimes on blue, sometimes on white paper. Then these were taken home and the line work was added either with charcoal or crayon or Indian ink[2] There is another note, coming from the mother of Foxley Norris, Julia, who sometimes when she was very young accompanied her grandfather on his sketching expeditions, and remembers that he always dampened his paper before working on it, and she mentions that "he did this when using charcoal as well." Her description continued mentioning another interesting point about some of these sketches and that is that figures – in some cases a little group of figures – and animals, were cut out in white paper, stuck on to the sketch in the appropriate place with gum, and then treated with brush or crayon to bring them into tone with the rest. Julia wrote:

" I have one or two examples of these in my possession, and many years ago I was told by one who had watched Dr. Monro at work, that he would take a great deal of trouble about the placing of these groups and figures, pinning them on to the drawing first in one place then in another until he satisfied himself as to their proper place in the composition. The same person who told me this also told me that in the case of at any rate, (of) some of the sketches, the outline was added with a stick of dry Indian ink, while the paper was still wet, and this is the only satisfactory explanation of the quality of the line work in many instances."

Hector Monro, another grandson, denied he had ever used charcoal. He wrote about visiting Monro at Bushey, where he "kept a tub of water by the door, with old pieces of paper and even half envelopes, soaking. When he was about to go out sketching, he seized a handful of these, still wet, and used them." This would seem to confirm what Monro's granddaughter Julia had seen, perhaps mistaking a stick of dry India ink for charcoal, especially since she was quite young at the time, and the effect of a thicker line on damp paper could be similar to charcoal in appearance.

Further proof again came from Hector Monro, who wrote in reply to an article in the *Connoisseur Magazine* from November, 1917, by A.K. Sabin, suggesting that Dr. Monro sometimes used charcoal in his drawings. Hector Monro wrote to the publishers, J. Palser & Sons, to say:

> "I never saw any drawing of my grandfather's when he used charcoal; as he was fully occupied by his profession, it was in the evenings only that he could give time to drawing and painting. He kept drawing paper and indeed sometimes bits of letters and envelopes, in a bath or pan of water, took them out as he wanted them, put them on a pad of blotting paper, wet as they were, made his outlines with a stick or piece of Indian Ink, and then the rest with a brush. There is no charcoal or chalk in them. I can prove this for I have scores of sketches, and when the paper was thin the paint had gone right through it. My cousin, Dr. Henry

Monro also told me this and as a young man he was often with his grandfather."

This seems to suggest that mental notes and rough drawings were made from nature during the day and the final versions touched up indoors of an evening. His subjects were usually rural scenes mainly of trees and foliage with a cottage or farm building. Sometimes, Hector Monro mentions that he added figures of people or animals cut out in white paper, stuck onto the drawing and then washed in to tone with the rest. He said that he took much time and care in putting these figures in just the right place, which is what we learn from Julia. Turner, in many of his early landscapes would add figures only at the last moment, sometimes disproportionately small, sometimes placed first as paper figures, to further enhance the picturesque qualities of a scene, perhaps a trick learned from Monro.

Sabin said that now and again Monro achieved by his method a misty luminosity which was astonishingly 'modern' in its result, and a number of varying effects, many of them fresh and pleasing and a few of them quite beautiful. He had a profound feeling for atmosphere, trees upon rising or receding ground, a little lake or pool, and now and again a cottage or ruined tower, and the diffused light of a distant sky, and these were the substance of nearly all of his drawings.[3]   Unlike this description, Turner by the age of twenty one was to give a clear imitation of the sense of drama that J.R. Cozens was able to infuse into his art. Monro did have access to Cozens' collection of drawings, both those he had completed and those he was still able to make for occupation. Turner is also thought to have had in his possession Cozens' watercolour of *Fluelen.* Between 1794 to 1798 Turner was also in constant contact with Sir Richard Colt Hoare, and saw his collection of eleven drawings by Du Cros, one of the most advanced artist pioneers, who is credited with influencing the style of Cozens. Following his years of close association with Monro, Turner was also at Fonthill working for Beckford both in 1799 and 1800. This additional opportunity of viewing the work of an artist he so admired, must have been a great opportunity for Turner to study the transformation of Cozens' work, partly resulting from his association with the Swiss painters in watercolour.[4] Turner also, thanks to Monro's influence, spent much time during the winter months of 1795 to 1796 teaching private pupils at Hadley. This is where the family of Monro's brother James lived, but other than a watercolour of their house, and of the local church, there seems to have been little kept of either Turner's efforts, or those of his pupils. Meanwhile Oppe was to write of Turner's amazing technique, where almost from the first he developed the utmost facility in brushwork, with a miniaturist's delicacy in his youthful architectural studies. He had a greater talent even that Girtin, he felt, in manipulating Girtin's expressive blots, and neither habit had left him. He had been trained in this accurate approach by the numerous drawings he had had to colour in whilst at Dr. Monro's of a winter evening. The blot technique which Girtin experimented with, must have come directly from Cozens, whose father Alexander, had his pupils at Eton use this technique.

The early period of Dr. Thomas Monro's life may be said to correspond with the rise and establishment of watercolours as a recognised medium, but how much he had to do with the foundation of the Old Society of Painting in Water-Colour is hard to prove. Certainly the standards and ideals which he insisted upon had much to do with the building up of the unrivalled position to which the English water-colour school attained. The early members of the Society owed much to his kindly help, teaching and criticism, to the extent that John Ruskin said of Monro that he was "Turner's true Master." The Society of Painters in

Water-Colours having been established, the main strength of the collection lay in its naturalistic landscapes, that were to become increasingly popular. Richard Ramsay Reinagle was the Treasurer of the Society by 1806, a friend to Girtin, and someone we know to have involved himself in the painting of panoramas.

Amateurs who flocked to the auction rooms and exhibitions to contend with each other for the purchase of pictures, recognised and demanded bravura of execution or exquisite daintiness of handling. Large pictures in watercolour were far from uncommon, for example Girtin's views of Harewood for his patron Lascelles, painted in 1801, measured about 25x38 inches, or 627x978 mm. Also at this time Richard Wilson again came into fashion, culminating in an exhibition of his work in 1814 at the British Institution, in which eighty four works by him were shown, along with a few pictures by Hogarth and Gainsborough. This new class of picture lover included many professionals and the newly rich merchants, who had originally lent pictures to establish the Institute, and who were also to prove to be Turner's new public, especially for engravings of his work. These men also collected the contemporary artists whose work was exhibited at the Institute, and were beginning to collect the new style of watercolour landscape.

The circle of young artists was very small, and there were many interconnecting links. Samuel Prout was a friend to William Hunt, David Cox and Peter de Wint. He was born in 1783 at Plymouth, and later had Benjamin Haydon as a friend. Prout, who died in 1852, used a broken line technique in his drawing, associated with those who graduated from the Monro school, influenced by Thomas Hearne. Haydon was often at the Adelphi, being a few years older than Prout, who would have been too young to have taken advantage of Monro's evening meetings.

Haydon was at Adelphi Terrace as a friend to Henry Monro, before he died, and he liked to draw from the works of Girtin, Turner and Cozens that could be found at the doctor's house, but was never a part of the evening meetings. We know that he had a fascination with Gainsborough's box, owned by the Monro family, was often coming over to watch it according to Tom, and this influenced him to experiment with the use of scientific aids, camera obscura for example, and Cornelius Varley's telescope. We hear nothing about David Cox having any connections other than friendship, but certainly John Varley had many connections with Monro, and it was he who the doctor persuaded to take on the young Linnell and William Henry Hunt as pupils.

We know how Hunt spent a good deal of time at Bushey, either with the Monros or with Lord Essex. He decorated at least one state room at Cassiobury for Lord Essex, and certainly assisted in the decorations of the dining-room there. Varley, we are told by Roget, "appreciated from the first his wonderfully delicate eye for colour". Hunt gained full membership of the Society in 1826, and the following year exhibited various studies of flowers, fruits and vegetables. Meanwhile as the doctor was preparing to move from his house in Adelphi Terrace, he appears to have used young John Linnell to sell some of his unwanted drawings. From Linnell's journal for 1820, recorded in his autobiography written in 1863, he wrote on 3rd February:

> "to Dr. Monro with Mr. Varley: brought away some drawings by Girtin, Cozens and co to show to Mr. Hall." The next day he wrote: "Mr. Hall came and bought a drawing by Girtin of Jedburgh, Roxburghshire for £14.14.0d. Paid. On 7th February he records; "Sent to C.Hall Esqre. at Southampton the two drawings by Girtin of Durham and York Minster. Price 15 gs. Separate of 26 gs. The two, making 40 for the three."

(Jedburgh, Durham and York)   Obviously there must have been some argument about the price, since Linnell then records on 10th: "to Dr. Monro who agreed to take 20 gs. for the two drawings by Girtin of Jedburgh and Durham.   Brought away two drawings by Cozens framed and glazed and 2 larger unframed."

The diary continues in this vein, with Linnell going back and forth collecting drawings from Monro, seemingly acting as middleman for a small profit. He recorded he was a frequent visitor, although by this time he can hardly have been a student. On 22nd he watched the 'Gainsboro Show' and brought away a folio of old drawings.   Obviously at this time Monro was indeed selling some of his old Girtin and Cozen's outlines, prior to moving out of the Adelphi, and it is interesting that he would use a former pupil as a contact to those who might be prospective buyers.   On 3rd March Linnel records that

"Sent to Dr. Monro the old drawings and all the remaining drawings by Cousins, Girtin and co unsold by Hammond Porter, who brought away for Mr. Varley a large frame and canvas."

The move to Bushey by the Monros seems to have led to Tom and his wife taking on the responsibility of having young Alexander come and live with his family on his return from France. Slowly the arrangements were falling into place, and the family had moved altogether by the end of the year of 1820. It had been a busy year, with the death of George III, who had expired at half-past-eight on 29th January, 1820. In July Monro seems to have experienced the excitement of the Coronation at first hand, when he came to town on 19th July. According to family tradition Monro and the Prince Regent, now George 1V, had played tennis together, and it was on one of these occasions that Monro had damaged his knee. This seems to have caused him problems for the rest of his life, and he generally preferred to ride rather than walk, sometime referring to the fact that his leg "felt like paste". He had been rewarded by George IV with a gold pencil, but perhaps that was poor compensation for a problem that was to be with him in old age. Less than a month after the Coronation Tom records that "Queen Caroline died, on August 7th at half past ten." She had never been acknowledged Queen by her husband, who, whatever her faults, seems to have treated her disgracefully.

Sally remained at home following the move to Bushey, still unmarried, having turned down a Major MacInnes, during the summer the family moved, who is mentioned as having been wanting to marry her. We do not know what her feelings must have been at this time, although Tom records that she had not been well, and he and his wife Sarah, in spite of having four children by then, Edward, Henry, Eleanor and Theodore, seem constantly to have made her welcome, and had her to dinner. Tom's family had by then moved to a much larger house at 33 Bedford Place, in January 1820, which was as well since Monro seems to have started his habit of coming to town at least once a month, and sometimes spending a night with Tom and Sarah. In spite of having retired, family problems were still a part of Monro's life, for Farington mentions in his diary that the doctor had called and spoken to him about his nineteen year old son, who had much pleasure in drawing and wished for improvement. Apparently his father applied to Reinagel Junior for that purpose, but he had asked £220 for three months board and instruction, whilst the doctor proposed £120. They do not seem to have come to any agreement. By 1821 Farington reported that John "is doing nothing at present", although he did appear to have had a studio at 13 Hadlow Street, probably before 1824. It has never been recorded as to whether he did manage to acquire some training. It does appear that John had a quick temper, was quite difficult and very independent, and even had a tendency to drink too much. Following the excitement of his elopement with Harriet Chitty, the couple were eventually married, lived a devoted and happy life, and John taught his wife to draw. They sold enough work to live on, until they received a small legacy after the doctor's death. There are many of John Monro's drawings still in existence, with softer outlines than those of his brother Alexander, but their subjects and style were very similar. John died in 1880.

Alex mainly made drawings of buildings and a few rural scenes at Bushey, Oxford, Albury, Surrey, Brighton, Malvern, Guernsey and the Isle of Wight. He died in 1844, leaving three more children by his second wife. Many of his drawings of buildings are recognised by the hard straight lines, sometimes even looking as if they had been drawn in with a ruler, when depicting such objects as chimney stacks or roof gutters. He lived with his son Donald at Bushey, remaining there until 1833, when Monro died. His second marriage to Lucy Agnew, seems to have brought him sufficient means to have enabled him to dispense with the necessity of working or selling pictures, although he did share a studio with this brother John.

When he retired to Bushey, it may be that the doctor was then finding leisure for drawing and painting, since he never dated his work, and it was probably during this period that a large portion of his enormous output was being created. Eventually the shadows of old age and ill health subdued his zeal, weakened his eyesight and limited his mind to the material things of the body and the visits of the chimney sweep and other domestic details, as recorded in his last diaries. The late Thomas Girtin, son of the artist, wrote that Monro's small sitting room at Bushey was "full of paint and stuffiness."[5] Monro was disorderly. His son Tom wrote that in the Adelphi days it was he who "arranged and cleaned Pa's books", suggesting that his father had little sense of tidiness in these matters, unlike Tom himself. There is also a description of a small octagonal room at Bushey, which was 'quite a little den, all fustiness and ill-lighted by a sky light', where the doctor spent much of his time in old age. Monro also rode to church in a loose wrapper, and is depicted by William Hunt dressed in such a fashion. He certainly rode out to sketch, and no doubt used the badly lit room as a studio of sorts, where he would finish his drawings. To the end of his life Monro continued to encourage young artists. In 1828, on the recommendation of John Varley, he invited Welby Sherman to stay with him at Bushey. In a letter to George Richmond that autumn, Samuel Palmer wrote with some characteristic touches of sarcasm:

"I suppose you know that Mr. Sherman is or has been with Dr. Monro at Bushey. He likes an artist to live with him, and work for him from the cottages etc. thereabout. He has some of the first rate housepainters and sky sloppers and bush blotters there. I fear Welby won't do for him not having the requisite facility....Mr. Sherman went recommended by Varley to Dr. Monro: he got there at night. Next morning he made a sketch of the Dr.'s house before breakfast. After breakfast two steeds were caparison'd, on one of which mounted the Dr. and on the other Discipulus, and set forward to depict from Nature. The Doctor led the way to that selected scene which he intended to commend first of all to his visitor's attention. It did not consist wholly of nature or wholly of art. Had we had the happiness of beholding it, how must it have rais'd our esteem and admiration for his taste who first discover'd and explored it...The picturesque tourists arrived at the Arcadia of their destination – and Behold it was a Brick Field! ! The Doctor's outline was soon done and he went home to tint it. Mr. S. remained several hours and made three sketches, one of which, when he came home in the evening the Doctor (who by this time had quite finished his own) kept: and politely informed Mr. Sherman that his carriage was going to town the next morning and he might if he pleas'd avail himself of that convenience – which he accordingly did."[6]

There is little in Tom's diary about the artistic side of his father's life, so it is quite revealing to have any mention of artistic pursuits. The social side of life continued, and many visits were made to Lord Essex, Charles Dance and other neighbours. Nothing is recorded of the doctor's reaction when Tom brought back into the family his brother Henry's picture of *Othello* which had been sold after Henry's death by his father to pay some of his son's debts. General Grant of Wimpole Street had bought it, and after several mentions in the diary about the General wanting his picture back after he had sold it to Tom, eventually there is an entry which mentions that Grant had given him the picture as a gift. The picture remains in the family to this day. There are a few letters from a correspondence between John Linnell and Monro from the year 1822 (Fitzwilliam Museum) when the artist wrote to the doctor to ask for one of Girtin's drawings done in York. We get a hint of the disorder of Monro's papers when he writes to say he cannot possibly find it at this time, and was 'perfectly indifferent' to parting with it. In another letter from August of that year, in another hand and possibly dictated to his daughter Sally, as it appears to be in her handwriting style, Monro writes to Linnell that his drawings he regards as "a bank note at any time, and thinks at any rate that he should not be disposed to take £10 for it." However they do seem to have remained friends, as Linnell also wrote to tell him about Sherman, and Monro suggested that he would take an early opportunity of calling on the artist on that subject, suggesting that he did still make the occasional trip to London.

The doctor himself took up his own diary, when on June 24th, 1824, he wrote: "This day I arrived at the age of 65 years, and finding this book in which I perceive at the beginning of the year 1811 I commenced writing. Why I left off I do not recollect or why I seem inclined to scribble and therefore have taken up my pen for the purpose, but what am I to say? I will say this – that I am greatly thankful to my merciful Creator for suffering me to live with a share of health tolerably good. I flatter myself that all my mental faculties are in as perfect a state as they ever were. When it is His pleasure to call me hence and be no more seen, of course I must like all other mortals submit. I am not anxious for a long life, but I am anxious for the possession of my mental faculties as long as I live and may Almighty God graciously grant that I may enjoy them. I have thro' life seen too much misery in consequence of the failure of human reason that I cannot but most ardently deprecate its taking place in my system. I am most thankful to divine Providence for all the excellent qualities evidently conspicuous in my eldest son. He is now the staff and prop of my life and seems to be so necessary to its support – that if any accident should deprive me of him I think I should not long survive it. I may truly say he is one of the most perfect – if not the most perfect human being capable (of?) enjoying. There is a mildness – lucidity of manner and deportment in him which is in every respect admirable and a good sense of propriety of conduct must ensure him to be the approbation of all who know him."[7]

The diary was not taken up again until 1828, when on September 7th Monro suffered the shock of the death of his wife Hannah. He wrote:

"Alas what Hiatus! How difficult it is for such a mind as mine to follow up what it sometimes points. What a loss to have sustained since last I wrote in this book! Nobody can possibly form a judgment of that loss – but those who have in a similar manner experienced a similar affliction- in their wives, and have had the misfortune to loose them. I am now bereft of that prop which under all the circumstances of vexation and disappointment used to afford me comfort above 40 years.

Sept. 11th: "The anniversary of my wedding day. It used to be a day of rejoicing and we generally had a number of friends to celebrate it but alas! Those days are all gone by and the Melancholy reflections which now harass my mind have taken the place of those cheerful hours I used to pass with my friends. I feel that I have lost that which never can be restored – my daughter Sally is kind and affectionate but her attentions and cares are too much divided to afford me that support which under all circumstances of Affliction I was sure to find in my dear, dear wife. My tears chase one another down my cheeks whilst I write this, and pangs of the deepest regret will ever be present to my mind whenever I reflect upon the loss of such unbounded affection as hers was."[8]

Tom reported in his diary that his mother was taken ill in September, and by December he travelled to Bushey with Dr. Hare. By the 5th January, 1828, his mother was dead, and was to be buried at Bushey church. Until this event the doctor's life had appeared to be fairly settled, with his son John finally getting married to Harriet, in 1826, whilst Sally had married her cousin Fred Monro. Robert, married to his cousin Charlotte, had a parish at Clifton, Bristol, whilst Alexander was at home as well. After his wife's death Monro bought a smaller house, but had appeared to do little with this. By 1832 he wrote again in his diary: "At length I have got into my own house which I some years ago built after the model in some measure of Fetcham. I have felt very unwell most of the time. I have inhabited it but my complaints, whatever they may be, seem disposed to an occasional amelioration." From that time his notes are mostly about family visits, he does have one entry of interest. For a sore throat he recommended: "Mix a pennyworth of camphor pounded with a wineglassful of brandy. Pour a small quantity on a lump of sugar. Allow it to dissolve in the mouth every hour. The 3rd or 4th dose generally enables the patient to swallow with ease."

For about three months following the death of his wife, a Major and Mrs. Newton appear to have stayed in the house with Monro, leaving by the end of January. The doctor wrote in his diary again:

"Termination of the Newtonian visit. I wish I could afford always to have them in my home".

This would suggest that the doctor was lonely, in spite of numerous visits of his children, grandchildren, especially Donald and Julia, the daughter of Robert and Charlotte. The last pages of his diary are much taken up with how much he paid his servants, for example £2.17shillings and ninepence to the Housemaid, with the Kitchen maid getting two pounds, and Samuel £3.3 shillings. There is even an entry mentioning that Fred (married to Sally) and Eddon (eldest son of Tom and Sarah) went to Town in the steam carriage and returned to dinner, so obviously this was a novelty, and exciting for the young boy. In the main Monro seems concerned with the weather, and his writings are dotted with sketches of chimney pots, suggesting that it was the domestic side of life that now concerned him. He admits that he is very weak and "can scarcely do the most trifling thing. I feel it impossible to combat this state of things much longer – if I do not get stronger." He dines with Sir Charles Dance on several occasions, otherwise compared to the old life, his social life is restricted, mostly to family who come and go. His old friend and onetime neighbour Henderson, came to dinner, with a Sir C. Scudamore. He mentions that he went to the Panorama of Milan,' but was not there for 5 minutes' before he was obliged to take his departure, so it would seems that some of his old problems were still with him. The doctor lived long enough to see a sale take place at the house Merry Hill, when many of his possessions were sold. Alexander must have decided to make many changes, and the small cottage which Monro named Clayhill, was not large enough to accommodate much in the way of furniture. He seems to have spent much time in his remaining years sorting out his extensive collection of drawings and engravings, since he left specific instructions in his will that these were to be sold, and only family drawings were to be retained and divided up. Having been accused by his critics of wanting to make money out of his famous pupils, it is interesting that in his collections were two volumes of original early Turner drawings. These he had at one time pasted into two volumes, which he kept until his death. Turner bought them back himself during the Monro sale, and eventually gave them, as part of the Turner bequest, to the British Museum.

The end when it came was sudden. His daughter was staying with him on 11th May, 1833, when he had a stroke, and his sons Tom, Robert and Alex, were summoned to his bedside. He died on 14th May, in his seventy third year, and was buried at Bushey churchyard by the graves of his wife, his son Henry and his old friends Hearne and Edridge. He lived long enough to see watercolour painting recognized as a serious branch of art. The Royal Society of Painters in Water Colour was by this time established in the Gallery in Pall Mall, and the National Gallery had already been established some ten years before Monro died.

If he left any other legacy, other than an extensive collection of engravings, it was in the form of the many students to whom he had imparted a love of nature, with all its seasonal changes, taken up in many different way by his various students with the most famous being Turner, with his ability to define movement and change and the ever changing light. Local Bushey artists were aware of his ideas of sketching and painting outdoors, and many followed his example. The last remark written in Monro's diary was on the view out of his window, with the two larches changing their leaves, and that he had never seen finer colouring. It is surprising that he remained so true to the style of his generations, preferring to draw only in line and wash, and seldom experimenting with colours. The suggestion from Samuel Palmer that he always had young artists with him may well have been true, although not a proven fact, but this certainly proved that his deepest interest lay in observing and depicting the world around him.

Edward Thomas and Robert were the Executors of his will. He left a chiming clock, his books, prints, pictures and drawings in his house to be divided among his children. Many of the drawings by Henry had already been sold in 1827. Monro stipulated that "these belongings may be divided amongst my children" and everything else in his collections was to be sold at Public Auction, or by private contract. The sale took place in 1833, lasting for five days. Brooke House, Clapton, being for the reception of lunatic patients, was to be left under the management of Tom, "so long as he shall continue personally to act in the conduct and management in full satisfaction and discharge –of the covenant entered into by me on his marriage with his present wife to securing to him the profits of my share of the established professional fees, and medical attendance as Physician to make up to him the annual sum of £350." Tom was to have the first refusal of buying any shares relinquished by any other member of the family. Finally Monro stipulated that shares "shall not be sold out of the family."

Dr Munro's sale was held at Christies in June and July 1833. It was described as 'a very capital collection of drawings of that well-known and intelligent collector of principal artists of the modern English school.' He had drawings by all the artists mentioned in this description, who attended his Friday sessions, as well as drawings by such old masters as Salvator Rosa, an historical picture by Rembrandt, several by Canaletto, a Titian landscape and 28 of Gainsborough's drawings. The sale raised £2,723 which was a considerable sum of money in those days. There was a drawing by John Varley inscribed *View from Polesden, near Bookham in Surrey, made in the company of Dr Munro, October 1800.* There was no mention of pencil drawings by Dayes made under that section in the Monro Sale Catalogue, but Turner acquired a number of them at the sale. It is possible they may have laid concealed among the number of miscellaneous sketches in the collections. There were over a hundred drawings of Antiquities and Buildings, of which Monro had consigned forty to a group by Turner as he attempted to sort his belongings in the previous year, but Girtin's grandson points out that these were the main sources from which the drawings on card were copied and may well have been by the hand of others. As he mentioned, with the cachet of Monro and the name of Turner attached, all these cards have descended as by Turner and will doubtless continue to do so unless more contemporary evidence is found. In addition Monro had over two hundred drawings by William Alexander, which he seems to have collected, as well as works by Hearne and Edridge.

Munro's influence lay mainly in giving young artists the opportunity to study his extensive collection of drawings.

He never gave them technical instruction as did his friends Hearne and Edridge, but advice, so his influence seems to have been from his friendship and encouragement and secondly in giving his pupils opportunity to study with skilled artists such as Edridge and Hearne and in bringing young men together so giving them the opportunity to learn from the talents of each other.

1. HenryEdridge's painting of Boulevard des Italiens from this date (V&A collections)
2. Foxley-Norris
3. Sabin – A.K. Connoisseur Mag. Nov 1917
4. Bell, C.F. Walpole Society Vol. XX111 1935 p22-23
5. Letter in the British Museum
6. Letter in the collection of the late Dr Jefferiss
7. Taken from a diary, in two slim volumes, in the collection of the late Dr. Jefferiss.
8. Letter in a private family collection
9. Diary in the collection of the Jefferiss family.

D

c

For detailed descriptions of the Monro sale see the Sale Catalogue held by the British Museum Library

LIST OF ILLUSTRATIONS

document of Turner's contact with Monro. Coloured watercolour. (family collec.)

6) Scene with Barn, by Thomas Monro (family collection) black ink on paper

7) Valley View with Houses by Thomas Monro (family collec.) Black ink and wash on paper

8) Trees on a Hill in a circular frame by Thomas Monro Black ink/charcoal on paper (family collec.)

9) View of London from Greenwich by John Varley (private collec.) coloured watercolour

10) Captain James Monro of Hadley by J. Downman, 1789 coloured chalk on paper in the collection of a family descendent.

11) Engraving of Dr. James Monro 1680-1752

12) Engraving of Dr. John Monro – father of Thomas

13) Engraving of Dr. Edward Thomas Monro – elder son, Born 1789 and known as Tom

14) Engraving of Dr. Henry Monro second son of Edward Thomas These four engravings are from a single picture showing five generations of doctors in the Monro family, including Thomas

15) Dr. Monro visiting his stables at Bushey after the fire by William Henry Hunt. Reproduced by kind permission of The Syndics of the Fitzwilliam Museum, Cambridge.

16) Landscape with a River by Thomas Monro, with kindpermission of the Ashmolean Museum, Oxford. Black ink and wash

17) Landscape with a Road by Thomas Monro, with kind permission of the Ashmolean Museum, Oxford.Black ink and wash

18) Landscape with a Church Tower by Thomas Monro, with kind permission of the Ashmolean Museum, Oxford. Black ink and wash

19) A view in the Wood by Thomas Monro, with kind permission of the Ashmolean Museum, Oxford. Black ink and wash
20) A coloured drawing by Thomas Monro of A Country Inn near a Pond, with kind permission of the Ashmolean Museum
21) Clandon Park, Surrey – 23rd June, 1827, by Alexander Monro Watercolour – private collection.

BIBLIOGRAPHY

Arts Council of Great Britain	John Sell Cottman V&A London (Box 0017)	1982
Bell, C.F.	Dr. Thomas Monro & James Moore Walpole Society Vol. 27 – Vol. 5 Thomas Jones, Walpole Soc. Vol.32	1936-8 1917 1946-8
Barrell, John	Painting and Politics of Culture Oxford University Press	1992
Binyon, Laurence	Thomas Girtin 1775-80 Seeley & Co. London	1900
Cave, Kathryn – Editor	The Diaries of Joseph Farington 1807-1816 Yale University Press, New Haven. U.S.A	1984
Chenevix Trench	Charles The Royal Malady Longmans Group UK Ltd	1964
Croft-Murray, E	British Museum Quarterly – Vol.X	1935-36
Dayes, Edward & Brayley	The Works of the late Edward Dayes	180
Gage, John	Colour in Turner: Poetry & Truth Studio Vista, London	1969
Garlick, K Macintyre and Angus	Editors Vol.1 – 1793 to Vol.12 – 1813 The diaries of Joseph Farington Vols.7-16 edited by Kathryn Cave Yale University Press, New Haven	1978-84
Girtin, Thomas with David Loshak	The Art of Thomas Girtin A & C Black – London	1954
Harman, Claire	Fanny Burney Harper Collins, London	2000

Jefferiss, F.G.	Biography of Thomas Monro – typed See Exhibition Catalogue at V&A	1976
Kriz, Kay Dian	The Idea of the English Landscape Painter Yale University Press, New Haven & London	1997
Leslie, C.R	Memoirs of the Life of John Constable London (V&A Library	1845
Lindsay, Jack	Turner: His Life and Work Granada Books, London & New York	1973
	Gainsborough: His Life and His Art Granada Publishing – London, New York	1982
Oppe, A.P	The Water-Colour Drawings of John Sell Cotman The Studio, London Water-colours of Turner, Cox & De Wint Halton & T. Smith – London & New York	1923 1925
Owen, Felicity	Collector of Genius: The Life of Sir George Beaumont Yale Univ. Press, New Haven, U.S.A	1988
Porter, Roy	A Social History of Madness Wiedenfield & Nicholson, London	1987
Pyne, W.H	Observations on the Rise and Progress of Painting in Water-Colour Repository of Arts – April	1813
Redgrave, Samuel	Dictionary of Artists of the English School George Bell & Sons, York St. Covent Garden	1878
Roget, John Lewis	A History of the Old Water-Colour Society London, Longmans, Green & Co. Vol.1	1891

Sloan, Kim	Alexander & John Robert Cozens	
	Exhibition Catalogue for the V&A-1986	
	Art Gallery of Ontario, Toronto	1987
	The Poetry of Landscape	
	Alexander & John Robert Cozens	
	Yale University Press	1986
Wilton, Andrew	British Watercolours 1750-1850	
	Turner 1775-1851	
	The Tate Gallery, London	1974

The British Museum holds three boxes of papers and letters on the Monro School, once in the possession of Julia Coode, (Thomas's grand-daughter) given by Mr. P.D.O. Coryton. Ref. c.167.6.26.27

The diaries were in the possession of Harold Coode, were copied by Elmira Wade, and referred to for the Exhibition catalogue by Dr. Jefferiss (V&A – 1976) The letter from Samuel Palmer is now held by a grandson of Dorothy Curtis Hayward (Thomas's grand-daughter)

Front Cover. Thomas Monro F.R.C.P. Fifth son of Dr. John Monro,
By John Downman – 1788

Mrs. Hannah Monro, daughter of Rev. Woodcock
By John Downman – 1788

Back Cover. Bethlem Hospital – in the collection of the Thomas
Coram Foundation
By Edward Haytley

Frontispiece. Dr. Thomas Monro – portrait by his son Henry Monro
By permission of the Royal College of Physicians of
London, where it now hangs.